FUN
WITH
STRING⋆

A collection of string games, useful
braiding & weaving, knot work & magic
with string and rope

by JOSEPH LEEMING
Illustrated by Charles E. Pont

DOVER PUBLICATIONS, INC
NEW YORK

Published in Canada by General Publishing Company, Ltd., 30 Lesmill Road, Don Mills, Toronto, Ontario.

Published in the United Kingdom by Constable and Company, Ltd.,

This Dover edition, first published in 1974, is an unabridged and unaltered republication of the work originally published in 1940 by J. B. Lippincott Company.

International Standard Book Number: 0-486-23063-5
Library of Congress Catalog Card Number: 74-75260

Manufactured in the United States of America
Dover Publications, Inc.
180 Varick Street
New York, N.Y. 10014

FOREWORD

EACH and every one of us sees or uses pieces of string nearly every day. There are very few, however, who have been initiated into the wonderland of fascinating things that can be done and made with this commonplace article of daily use. Once one does discover the different things that can be made and the games that can be played with string, a new world is opened up. Anyone who once contracts a genuine case of "string fever" will have little difficulty in amusing himself or interesting others. Time will rarely hang heavy on his hands, as long as a piece of string is available.

Some of the string crafts, such as square knot work, weaving, and braiding, will provide some interested readers, it is hoped, with a life-long hobby. Square knot work, in particular, with which an almost unlimited number of designs can be produced by combining the different methods of knotting, is one of the most fascinating of all the handicrafts, and one that is as yet but little known or practiced in this country.

It is believed that this represents the first attempt that has been made to gather together in a single volume all, or nearly all, of the various crafts, games, knots, and other occupations and pastimes that involve the use of string. Heretofore this information has been scattered throughout numerous books, a number of which have not been published or been generally available in the United States. The author hopes most sincerely that the collection presented in this volume will afford its readers, both young and old, many happy hours of interest and entertainment.

JOSEPH LEEMING.

CONTENTS

STRING GAMES AND FIGURES

FUN WITH STRING

MAGIC WITH STRING AND ROPE

THE DISSOLVING STRING

Ask one of your friends, a girl, to lend you a bracelet for this trick, or, if no bracelet is available, get a curtain ring or some other ring having a diameter of 3 to 4 inches. Then ask one of your spectators to tie the two ends of a piece of stout cord around your two wrists. The cord should be about 2½ feet long, so its length between your wrists will be about two feet.

Now take the bracelet or ring in your hand and inform the audience that you propose to dissolve the string by magic. Turn your back to the onlookers for a moment and, when you turn around again, the ring is on the string between your wrists. It can be removed by cutting the string or, if you prefer, you can turn your back to the audience and remove it by the secret magic method of "dissolving the string."

The bracelet or ring used for this trick must be large enough to slip easily over your hand. To get it onto the string, slip it over your right hand, passing it under the loop of string encircling your right wrist. Then, by passing the ring back over your right hand and fingers, it will be threaded on the string between your wrists. To remove the ring, simply reverse the process. Pass the ring over your right hand; and then slip it under the loop of string on your right wrist, and pull it free over your right hand and fingers.

HAND IN POCKET

Ask one of your friends to remove his coat and, when this has been done, hang a long piece of string with ends tied together to form a loop, over his right arm. Then tell him to put his right hand in his right waistcoat pocket, and see if he can remove the string without taking his hand from his pocket. If your friend is unsuccessful, which is practically certain to be the case, ask him to loop the string over your arm, and show him how it is done.

The procedure is as follows: Push the string through the right

1

armhole of your waistcoat, draw the loop over your head, and then push it through the left armhole of your waistcoat and put your left arm through the loop. The string will now encircle your body, and, by simply drawing it down to your feet, you can step out of it.

If you are not wearing a waistcoat, you can put your right hand in your trousers pocket. The procedure for removing the string is the same as described above, except that the string does not have to be pushed through the armholes of the waistcoat.

THE TWO CAPTIVES

THIS trick can be included in a program of string and rope magic, or can be used, with very hilarious results, as a party game. When exhibited as a feat of magic, the magician first ties the ends of a piece of string loosely around the wrists of one of the people in the audience. He then ties one end of another piece of string around his own left wrist, and passes the string in back of the piece joining the spectator's wrists. Then he ties the free end of his string around his own right wrist as shown. Hey, presto! The magician makes a

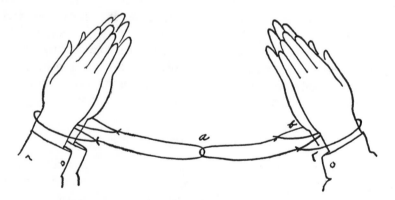

swift movement and in the twinkling of an eye has freed his string from that of the other person. To all appearances, one string has passed right through the other.

The trick is done as follows: The magician takes the center of the piece of string tied to his own wrists and passes it over the other person's left hand until it reaches the wrist. He then pushes it under the string encircling the other person's wrist, draws on it, and it comes away free of the other person's string.

To make a party game of the trick, fasten several pairs of boys and girls together. Then the game is to see which pair can first find out how to separate themselves. If no one is able to discover the secret after a reasonable length of time, it is up to the host to show it to them so they can get free of their bonds.

THE CUT AND RESTORED STRING (1)

THIS is a favorite method with many magicians of performing the famous cut and restored string trick. It is a good method to learn because it requires no preparation and is very easy to execute.

Show a piece of string about two feet long to the audience and ask them to examine it to make sure that it is free of preparations of any kind. When it is returned, tie the two ends together to form a loop. Grasp the ends of the loop in your two hands and give it a single twist to make the string cross itself at the center of the loop. Take hold of the point at which the string crosses itself with the thumb and forefinger of the left hand and place both ends of the loop in your right hand. The string will now be linked as shown in the illustration.

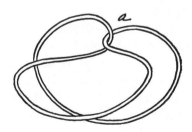

Now cover point A, where the string crosses itself, with the thumb and fingers of your left hand and grasp the string with the right hand about an inch or so away from point A. Then ask one of the audience to cut through the section of string between your hands with a pair of scissors or a knife. Apparently, the string is being cut in two pieces, but in reality only one end of the loop is cut off. Pull the ends of the string apart and show the audience that it is still a single piece.

The effect of this trick can be very greatly increased by first forming a loop, having it cut through, and showing the audience the result, namely, the division of the string into two pieces. To do this, twist the string as shown in the illustration but, instead of grasping point A, hold the double-looped string at other points. Then, when the section between your hands is cut, the string will be divided into two separate pieces.

THE CUT AND RESTORED STRING (2)

THIS is another method of doing the cut and restored string trick that is preferred by some magicians, amateur and otherwise. In this version of the trick a single length of string about a yard long is used instead of a loop.

Take one end of the string between the thumb and forefinger of each hand. Then ask some member of the audience to hand you the center part of the string. Take this part between the second and third fingers of each hand, opening these fingers like a pair of scissors so the spectator can put the string between them. Hold the hands about 3 or 4 inches apart.

Now comes the secretly executed part of the trick. Release the part of the string that is held between the second and third fingers of the left hand and with those fingers grasp the end piece of the string held in the right hand. As you do this, shift the right-hand end piece from between the thumb and forefinger to between the second and third fingers of the right hand. The right-hand end of the string will now extend between your hands in the position occupied a moment before by the center portion of the string.

Turn your right side toward one of the spectators and ask him to cut through the string that is stretched between your hands. The turning movement is made so the right-hand end of the string, which is now in back of the left hand, will not be noticed. When the string has been cut, conceal the end that has been cut off in your left hand, and pass the remainder of the string to the audience for their inspection.

When doing this trick the spectator who is to do the cutting should be hurried as much as possible without exciting suspicion, so he will not have time to examine the exact arrangement of the string too closely. Futhermore, it is well to say, "Cut the *center* part of the string, between my hands," thus recalling to the audience minds that the center portion has just been placed between your hands.

THE MAGIC LOOPS

THIS is a most baffling bit of string magic which, like many other good tricks, can be repeated over and over again, and becomes more puzzling with each repetition.

The two ends of a piece of string about three feet long are tied together to form a loop. The magician then forms two inner loops inside the large loop in the manner described below. One of the spectators is asked to put his forefinger through the inner loop on the magician's left. He does so; the magician pulls the string with his right hand, and the loops tighten and bind themselves around the spectator's finger.

The loops are formed again, precisely as before, and the magician inserts his own left forefinger in the left-hand inner loop. He pulls the string with his right hand and, instead of binding around his finger, it seems to pass right through it, leaving his finger free.

The trick can be repeated as many times as desired; yet each time the result is the same, unless the magician wishes to vary the performance and make the string pass through the spectator's finger as it does his own.

The method of forming the inner loops is made clear by the illustrations. Figs. 1 and 2 show how to make the loops when you wish the string to pass through the finger inserted in the left-hand inner loop. Take up the lower string at A between your right thumb and forefinger. Then take the string at the point marked B, Fig. 2, between your left thumb and forefinger, passing them, as shown by the dotted line, across the side of the string nearest to you. Stretch your hands apart, and put the loops on the table. Withdraw your hands from the string, before inserting your forefinger in the left-hand inner

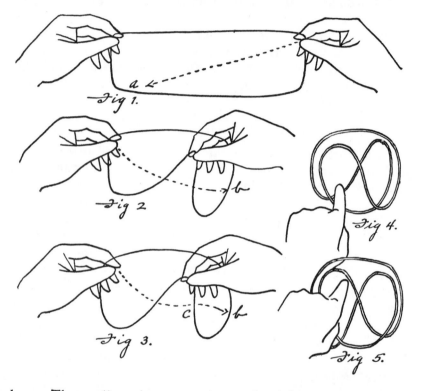

Fig 1.

Fig 2

Fig 3.

Fig 4.

Fig 5.

loop. Then pull on the outer string at the right, and the two left-hand loops will pass through your finger. Fig. 4 shows the loops arranged for this way of doing the trick.

To make the loops so they will entrap the finger inserted in the left-hand inner loop, take up the string at point A as before, but in picking up point B, pass your left hand across point C on the side of the string that is away from you. When this is done, the two left-hand loops will close around the inserted finger when the outer right-hand string is pulled. Fig. 5 shows how the loops are arranged.

FINGERS AND THUMBS

THIS is one of the trickiest and most deceptive of all the string tricks. It looks so simple that every one else will want to try it, but not one in a hundred will be able to do it, until you tell them the exact movements required.

The magician takes a piece of string about 6 inches long and ties the two ends together to form a loop. He then puts it around his two forefingers, as shown in the illustration, and revolves his forefingers rapidly several times, one around the other. Stopping the revolving motion, he places the forefinger and thumb of each hand together as shown in the second drawing. The hands are then moved so the right forefinger and left thumb are uppermost. The tip of the right forefinger is placed against the tip of the left thumb, and the tip of the left forefinger is placed against the tip of the right thumb. Now raise the right forefinger and left thumb, as in the third drawing, and the string will be released and will fall clear altogether of the fingers and thumbs.

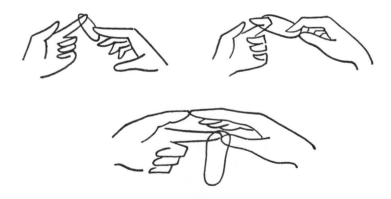

Once the method of doing this little sleight is mastered, it is simplicity itself; but, to realize its deceptiveness, try to teach it to someone else. Very often, the harder they try, the more confused they become.

THE NOSE AND STRING TRICK

THIS is another one of the string tricks that looks easy, but when people try to do it, they will usually fail because they do not make the small loop in the string the right way. The trick is done with a loop of string with a smaller loop at one end. When making the small loop, hold a 6-inch length of the string between the thumb and forefinger of each hand and double the part held by the right hand over that held by the left. This makes the right-hand part of the string the uppermost strand of the loop, as shown in the illustration, and it is essential that this be so if the trick is to succeed.

Now grasp the string between your teeth at the point marked A, and insert your left forefinger through the larger loop at point C, and pull the string taut. Put your right forefinger from below upward in the small loop at B. Crook your finger and bring the small loop down and out to the right of the large loop. Pass it over the right-hand string of the large loop and under the left-hand string, and then put the tip of your right forefinger, still inserted in the small loop, against the end of your nose. Open your teeth and pull the point C with your left hand, and the string will apparently pass right through your right forefinger.

THE RING AND STRING TRICK

TIE the two ends of a piece of string together to form a loop and then pass the loop through the center of a finger ring borrowed from some member of your audience. Then ask one of the spectators to hold up both forefingers and place the ends of the loop over them. The problem now is to remove the ring from the string without taking the string from the spectator's fingers.

This is done as follows: Grasp the string that forms the side of the loop nearest to the spectator's body, taking hold of it just to the right of the ring. Loop this string over the spectator's right forefinger, being careful to start the loop on the side of the finger that is on the outside, or away from the spectator's body. In other words, the loop is made by passing the string around the finger from front to back. Now lift off the loop that was originally around the spectator's right forefinger and the ring will be released.

THE SCISSORS AND STRING TRICK

THIS is another trick of the same kind as the "Ring and String" trick, but the method used to free the scissors from the string is a different one from that used in releasing the ring.

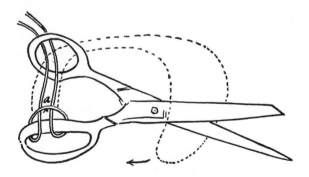

A pair of scissors is threaded onto a looped string in the manner shown in the illustration, and the free end of the loop is given to one of the spectators to hold. The problem is then to remove the scissors, and this is done as follows. Grasp the string at the point marked A, and pass this part of the string through the upper handle, around the blades and around the handles, as shown by the dotted line. The string will then slip right through the handles of the scissors and they will be released.

THE STRING IN THE BUTTONHOLE

THE magician takes a piece of looped string, passes it through one of the buttonholes in his coat, and puts his two thumbs through the loops at each end. Then, by apparently just pulling his hands apart, the string is freed from the buttonhole, precisely as though it had passed magically through the cloth of the coat!

This excellent little bit of string magic is done as follows: When your thumbs are in place, one at each end of the loop of string, hook the little finger of your right hand under the right-hand string of the loop that passes around the left thumb. Next hook the left little finger under the corresponding string of the loop that passes around your right thumb. Slip your right thumb out of its loop and put it through the loop held by the right little finger. When the thumb is in place, withdraw the right little finger. Then let the left little finger release the part of the string it is holding, and draw your two hands rapidly apart. The string will come free of the buttonhole, to all appearances passing right through the fabric of your coat.

Although the explanation of the different moves is of necessity somewhat long, the trick is carried out in a split second, once the moves have been learned.

THE DISSOLVING KNOT

TAKE a piece of string about 15 inches long, make a single knot in its center, and then tie the two ends together. The string will then be in the form of a figure 8, as shown in the illustration. Now ask one of your friends to see if they can untie the knot in the center of the string without untying the two ends. No one will be able to do it, but when you know the secret you can make the center knot dissolve away as quick as a flash.

The trick is very easy to do; but your audience does not know this, and the effect is always very mystifying. When you are ready to dissolve the knot, turn your back or else ask someone to throw a hand-

kerchief or napkin over your hands. Then simply grasp the center knot and slide it up to the knot that joins the two ends of the string. The center knot will merge with the end knot so it cannot be seen, and the string will form a simple loop instead of a figure 8.

THE LACED FINGERS

THIS is a very deceptive string trick in the sense that it appears easy to do, and yet will baffle anybody who tries to follow your mo-

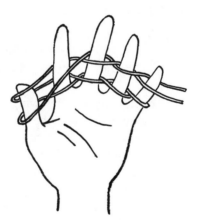

tions and perform the trick successfully. A piece of string is knotted to form a loop and is then laced around the fingers and thumb of the left hand in the manner shown in the illustration.

The lacing is done as follows: Hold the left hand out with the palm upwards and slip one end of the looped string over the left little finger. Cross the front string of the loop over the back string, and slip the two strings over the third finger. Repeat the process with the remaining two fingers, each time being sure to cross the front string over the back string. The illustration makes this clear.

The strings are now passed around the thumb and over the first finger. Study the drawing carefully to see just how this is done, for many people go wrong at this point by permitting the strings to cross each other as they go around the thumb. Note that the back string is uppermost, or nearest the top of the thumb, and is placed in back of the first finger.

When lacing the string back over the fingers, the front string is crossed over the back string in between the fingers, just as before. When the lacing is completed, slip the thumb free of the strings that pass around it and pull on the opposite end of the string with your right hand. The string will then apparently pass right through your fingers and will come completely free of them.

THE STRING THROUGH THE FINGERS

THIS is another trick of the "Laced Fingers" type in which a looped string, having been wound around the fingers and thumb, is pulled clear of the hand as though the flesh and bone were magically and momentarily dissolved.

The first step in the present trick, after tying the two ends of the string together to form a loop, is to place the string over the palm of the left hand, with the loop hanging down in back of the hand. Grasp the loop with the right hand and bring it over the left hand from back to front, the two strings forming the sides of the loop passing between the first and second fingers and the third and little fingers, as in Fig. 1. Next take strings A and B and pass them around the left thumb as in Fig. 2. String B is then crossed under string A and is passed from front to back between the third and little fingers. This is shown in Fig. 3. String A is passed from front to back between the first and second fingers, around the first finger from right to left, and is brought across the palm of the hand when the string will be arranged as in Fig. 4.

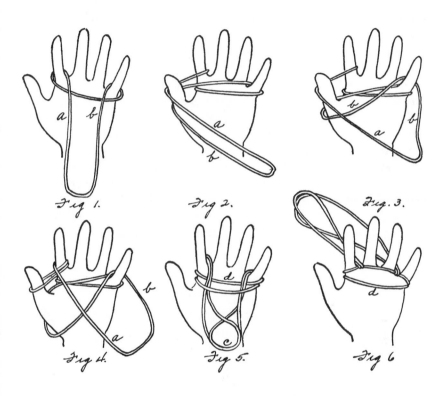

Fig 1. Fig 2. Fig. 3.

Fig 4. Fig 5. Fig 6

Now lift off the two strings that pass around the left thumb and pull them toward you as far as they will go. This will draw the loop shown in Fig. 4 up to the base of the four fingers and the string will appear as in Fig. 5. Put your right forefinger through the loop at point C and pass the loop from front to back over the fingers of the left hand (Fig. 6). Then pull the string D, Fig. 6, toward you, and the entire loop of string will come clear of your hand.

THE MAGICALLY TIED KNOT

THE magician produces a piece of string about 2 feet long and asks one of his spectators to tie the ends around his two wrists. A single length of string then extends from one wrist to the other. Turning his back for a moment, the magician then faces the spectators again. By some magical means a knot has been tied in the middle of the string!

This mystifying knot is tied in the following manner: Grasp the center of the string with both hands and form a loop by crossing the string over itself. Hold the loop between your right thumb and forefinger at the point where the strings cross, and push the loop under the string encircling the left wrist, starting on the lower side of the wrist and pushing the loop toward the left fingers. Then slip the loop over the left hand, bring it down to the back of the left wrist, and push it under the string encircling that wrist. Bring it up along the back of the left hand and pass it over the left fingers from back to front. Draw your two hands apart and the knot will be tied in the middle of the string.

THE STRING AND STRAW TRICK

THIS is a most excellent little trick which, if carefully practiced and executed, will be certain to make your friends believe that you are a real magician. A piece of string about 12 or 15 inches long is

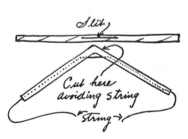

passed for examination and is then threaded through an ordinary drinking-straw. The magician bends the middle of the straw so it forms an acute angle and then cuts through the straw at the point of the angle with a pair of scissors. It is obvious to everyone that the string must also have been cut in two, yet, when the two halves of the straw are drawn apart, the string is discovered to be entirely whole and in a single piece as at the beginning!

The secret of the trick lies in the way in which the straw is prepared prior to the performance. As shown in the illustration, a slit about 2 inches long is cut in one side of the straw at its center. When the string has been threaded through the straw and the latter is bent, the slit should be on the inner side of the angle formed by the bending. The string is pulled tight and thus its center part is brought down through the slit, as shown. Care must be taken to keep this part of the string concealed by the left hand, which holds the center of the straw while the right hand is wielding the scissors. The straw is cut through, but the string is, of course, left entirely unharmed.

STRING FROM NOWHERE

THE magician holds out both his hands and exhibits them front and back to show that they are absolutely empty. Then, to make deception doubly difficult, he pulls up his coat sleeves, to show that nothing is hidden underneath his cuffs or up his sleeves. This done, he holds out his right hand, closed to make a fist. His left hand approaches it and slowly draws from within it a seemingly endless piece of colored string.

This excellent trick is very simply done. Prior to the performance, roll up a piece of string several yards in length and fasten to one end of it a glass bead or a small button. When you are ready to do the trick, secrete the rolled-up string under a fold of your coat sleeve in the crook of the left elbow. After showing both hands empty, pull up your right coat sleeve using, naturally, the left hand to do so. Then, with the right hand, pull up your left sleeve, grasping it at the elbow and gaining possession of the hidden string. Now, everything is ready for the amazing appearance of the string. Grasp the bead or button attached to the end of the string with the fingers and thumb of your left hand and pull the string out, keeping your movements slow to make the string seem as long as possible.

THROUGH THE FINGERTIPS

ASK one of your friends to hold out his left forefinger and when he does so, hang a loop of string over it. Hold the lower end of the loop in your own left hand. Then cross the left string over the right one, so the strings are as shown in Fig. 1.

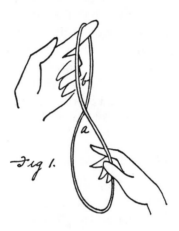

Turn your right hand so the palm faces to the left. Put your right middle finger between the strings at the place marked a, Fig. 1, and put your right forefinger, from below, between the strings at b.

Keeping the two fingers in position between the strings, turn your right hand palm downward. Place the tip of your right middle finger on the tip of your friend's forefinger, remove your right forefinger from its loop, and pull on the strings with your left hand. Presto! The strings slip right through both your friend's finger and your own, coming away free in your left hand.

THE RING MAGICALLY KNOTTED ON A STRING

PRODUCING a piece of stout string or cord about 3 feet long, the magician asks some member of the audience to tie its ends securely around his wrists. When this has been done, a single piece of string about two feet long will extend from one of the magician's wrists to the other.

Next the magician asks that someone lend him a finger ring. The magician holds the ring in his right hand and turns his back for a moment or two. When he turns to face the audience again, the ring is seen to be securely knotted to the center of the string! Indeed, the string has to be untied before the ring can be unknotted and removed.

This excellent string magic is done as follows: As soon as you turn your back, push the center of the length of string between your wrists through the ring, thus forming a loop. Slip the loop over your right hand and wrist to a point closer to the elbow than the string already encircling the wrist. Then bring it back underneath the string encircling the wrist and slip it back over the right fingers, passing it from the back of the hand to the front. The ring will then be tightly knotted to the center of the string.

THE VANISHING KNOTS

IN THIS trick three knots are tied in a piece of heavy cord, manila rope or clothes rope. The magician covers the knots with a handkerchief, blows upon them, and asks two spectators to pull on the ends

of the rope. The handkerchief is lifted, and the knots are found to have completely disappeared!

The accompanying illustration shows how the knots are tied. The first knot tied is the lower left-hand one shown in the figure. The second knot is tied above this with the ends crossing in the opposite direction as shown. The third "knot" is made by passing the right end down and through the lower knot from front to back, then up through the upper knot from front to back.

Now, when the ends are pulled apart, the rope will come out straight, free from knots.

THE KNOTTED ROPE

A PIECE of rope about 12 or 15 feet long is used in this trick. The magician, while calling attention to the fact that the rope is an ordinary one, not prepared in any manner, gathers it up in a number of loose coils around the left hand, and then tosses it out. Again the magician coils up the rope, and this time one of the spectators is asked to catch hold of the end of the rope when it is thrown out.

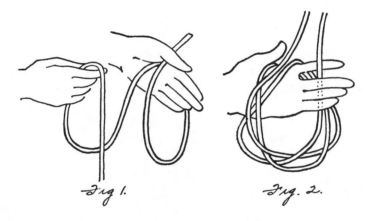

Fig. 1.   Fig. 2.

When the rope has been thrown, it is found that it has mysteriously tied itself in a dozen or more knots, which are spaced at equal distances along the rope.

A soft pliable rope should be used, and it is coiled over the left hand as indicated in Fig. 1. The coils are, as a matter of fact, a series of half hitches. To make these, hold the rope across the palm of the right hand, with the palm downward and fingers closed over the rope. Leave enough slack between the hands to form the next coil. Bring the right hand toward the left, at the same time turning it over so that the back of the right hand touches the wrist of the left hand. Put the left fingers under the rope passing across the back of the right hand and take off the coil that has been formed. A little practice will make this method of coiling clear and easy to do.

When you have made the last coil, grip the free end of the rope between the first and second fingers of your left hand, as in Fig. 2. Grasp the opposite end of the rope in your right hand and toss it toward the spectator. As the coils pass from your left hand, the end will be drawn through them, as it is firmly held between the left-hand fingers. Each coil will then be converted into a knot, which is drawn tight by the weight of the rope.

THE DECAPITATION ROPE TRICK

Two pieces of thin rope are exhibited by the performer, and passed around his neck. They are tied in a single knot in front.

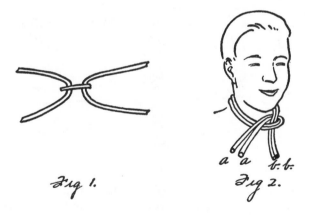

Fig. 1.   Fig. 2.

Presto! The performer pulls on the cords, which come free, having apparently been drawn right through the neck.

The ropes are prepared by tying them together at their centers

by a piece of thread or wool of the same color as the rope (Fig. 1).
When the ropes are being exhibited, their centers are kept concealed
by the performer's hand.

Pass the ropes around your neck, so their centers are at the back.
Be careful not to cross the ropes when you bring them to the front
and tie them in a single knot (Fig. 2). To make the ropes come free,
grasp the two top cords, A and A, in one hand, and the two bottom
cords, B and B, in the other hand and pull. The thread will break
and the cords will come free.

THE DISSOLVING LOOPS

THE performer exhibits two pieces of rope, as in Fig. 1. He
asks a spectator to take the ends of one rope, as A and A, and to tie
them together over the back of the hand. Another spectator is then
asked to take the ends of the other rope, B and B, and to tie them

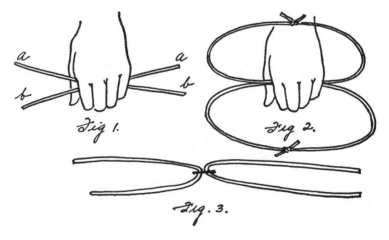

together beneath the hand (Fig. 2). The two spectators are then
asked to take hold of the loops. As soon as this is done, the performer
removes his hand. To their great surprise, the spectators are left
holding a single loop between them!

The trick is done by using two ropes fastened together at their
centers with a piece of thread, as in Fig. 3. The hand conceals this

join when the ropes are being exhibited at the beginning. When the ropes are tied as described, they form one large loop as soon as the thread is broken, which is accomplished by asking the spectators to pull out on the sides of the loops.

THE CHEVALIER ROPE ESCAPE

THIS trick, which was originated by the French magician Chevalier, may truly be described as sensational. Read the directions carefully and practice each step until you are letter perfect, and you will be able to puzzle your friends in no ordinary fashion.

The performer shows the audience two short pieces of rope, which he pulls upon to show that they are whole and untampered with. He passes the two ropes, placed side by side, around his waist and asks a spectator to tie them tightly together at the back. A third rope is then taken from the performer's table, passed around his neck, and tied at the back.

Two shorter ropes are then tied tightly around each wrist, after which the performer sits down on a chair which is placed sidewise to the audience. He then asks a spectator to tie the rope at his waist to the back of the chair and, when this has been done, to tie the ropes around his neck and wrists to the chair.

"Now," says the performer, "I propose to show you something rather extraordinary. In most rope escapes, the performer goes behind a screen or into a cabinet to make his escape. In this one, however—"

He does not finish the sentence. Instead, he suddenly stands up. He is absolutely free of the ropes, having apparently passed right through them, for they are all still firmly tied to the chair!

The rope recommended for this trick is soft cotton rope about ½ inch in diameter. If this cannot be obtained, clothes rope or manila rope will do. Cut four pieces about 4 feet long, and cut four more pieces about 2½ feet long.

Take two of the 4-foot pieces and tie them together at their center points with a piece of white thread (Fig. 1). Tie the remaining two 4-foot pieces together in the same way, and do the same with the two sets of 2½ foot pieces.

Prepare the two shorter sets and one of the longer sets by taking both ends of the same rope and holding them in the same hand, so the ropes are held together at their center points by the thread (Fig. 2). The remaining longer set is not arranged in this way until later.

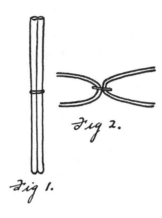

Fig 2.

Fig 1.

Lay the ropes over the back of a chair in the following order from left to right—first, the unprepared longer set; next the longer set prepared as in Fig. 2, and then the two shorter sets, each prepared as in Fig. 2.

Take up the first unprepared set of ropes 4 feet long and pull on them. Hold them in the right hand with the hand covering the thread at the center. When the pulling is finished, separate the ropes so they are as in Fig. 2. This movement can be covered by lowering the ropes momentarily on your right side and turning this side away from the audience. Now turn your back to the audience, pass the ropes around your waist, and ask a spectator to tie them at the back. The center of the ropes will pass beneath the bottom of your vest and be concealed.

The remaining set of 4-foot ropes is tied in the same manner around your neck, the join being concealed beneath your shirt collar. Take up one of the short sets, place it around your left wrist, and hold it while the spectator ties it on top of your wrist. The center is kept beneath your wrist and is covered by your right hand. The remaining short set of ropes is tied around your right wrist in the same manner. You now seat yourself and all four sets of ropes are tied to the chair.

While you are talking to the audience, as already described, strain against the ropes to get them under a slight tension, then, when you are ready to stand up, they will break at once, and you will be free.

THE BOUND-WRIST ROPE ESCAPE

IN THIS favorite rope escape, the magician's wrists are bound together with a handkerchief and a piece of rope about 10 or 12 feet long is passed between his wrists in back of the handkerchief. Some member of the audience is then asked to hold the two free ends of the rope. In spite of the predicament in which he has been placed, the magician frees himself of the rope in less time than it takes to say "Jack Robinson."

The first step in doing this trick is to take care that the handkerchief is not tied too tightly around your wrists, since you will need a little space with which to work in freeing yourself. To get free of the rope, once this precaution has been observed, first edge the part of the rope that passes between your wrists up between the palms of your hands. Push it in the right direction with one of your wrists, and then draw it along with your fingers. Then pass your right hand through the loop formed by the rope between your hands, step backwards, and the rope will slip off, passing between your right wrist and the handkerchief.

THE THUMB-TIE ESCAPE

THIS is a favorite "escape" trick with many professional magicians. They use a little metal collar that fits around the left thumb and permits the cord binding the thumbs together to be slipped off without difficulty. The method described here does not require any apparatus, but is just as effective and mystifying as that used by the professionals.

The magician crosses his right thumb over his left thumb, to form an X, and then asks some member of the audience to bind both thumbs together with a piece of stout smooth cord. No matter how tightly the cord is tied, the magician, by merely breathing upon the cord, causes it to dissolve. His thumbs come apart and he may put his arm through that of a person standing beside him or through a hoop, yet when he brings his hands together his thumbs are found to be tightly tied together as at the beginning of the trick. The knots are untied by one of the spectators to show that they have not been tampered with.

The secret of the trick is as follows: When approaching the person who is to tie your thumbs together, hold your two hands close together, with the cord passing across them, resting between the forefinger and thumb of each hand. Bring your hands together and cross your thumbs and, as you do so, bend your fingers inward and catch the central part of the string between the fourth and little fingers of each hand. The central part of the string will thus form a loop which is hidden by your fingers. After your thumbs have been bound together, you can get free in an instant by simply releasing this loop.

THE GREAT CHAIR ESCAPE

Two pieces of rope, each about 6 feet long, are used in this escape, which is a favorite with many performers who give "spiritualistic" exhibitions. They are examined by the audience to make certain that they are strong and whole from end to end, and are then tied to the magician's wrists. The end of one rope is tied around one wrist and the end of the other rope around the other wrist.

When this has been done, the magician seats himself on a chair, crosses his arms, and directs some member of the audience to tie the free ends of the two ropes to the rear legs or to the rungs of the chair. A screen is then placed in front of him and a moment later he commences to ring a dinner-bell that has been placed on the floor beside the chair, clap his hands together, throw tennis balls placed by the chair over the screen, and perform other "spiritualistic" feats requiring the use of one or both of his hands. When the exhibition is completed, however, and the screen is removed, the magician is found to be still tightly bound to the chair. The only plausible explanation appears to be that he really did summon a few spirits to carry out his commands, ring the bell, and so on.

This escape is, in reality, quite a simple one to execute. As soon as the screen has been put in place and the magician is hidden from the audience, he slides to the front edge of the chair seat and lifts his right arm over his head. Then, by turning around to face the chair, he can stand up and have all the freedom of movement necessary to carry out the various "demonstrations." When he is ready to have the screen removed, he simply slips back into his original position on the chair, and is then as tightly bound as at the beginning of the trick.

THE NECK AND KNEE ROPE TIE

THIS is a very interesting rope tie, escape from which appears to be impossible to those who do not know the secret. A piece of rope about 6 feet long is passed beneath the magician's right leg a little above the knee and arranged so the ends are of equal length on each side. A member of the audience then ties the rope with a single knot over the magician's leg and ties his right wrist on top of the knot. The left wrist is then tied on top of the right wrist and, the magician bending forward, the ends of the rope are passed around his neck and his head is tied down to his wrists. A screen is then placed in front of the magician and in a few moments he effects his release from the uncomfortable position in which he has been placed.

The escape is executed as follows: It will be noted that the first knot tied over the magician's leg is a simple knot. This can be made to slip along the rope. While the magician is being bound, he sits well forward toward the front edge of the chair with both feet on the rungs. This bulges out the upper leg muscles sufficiently so that, when the feet are removed from the rungs and straightened out, there will be considerable slack between his leg and the rope. The single knot is worked down on this slack part of the rope until the right hand is freed, and the remaining knots can be then rapidly and easily untied.

THE BEHIND-THE-BACK ROPE TIE

A PIECE of rope about 3 feet long is passed to the audience to be examined and, when everyone is satisfied that it is not secretly cut or weakened in any way, one of the spectators is asked to tie the center of the rope around the magician's right wrist. This done, the magician puts his right hand behind his back, places his left wrist over the knot on his right wrist, and asks the spectator to bind both wrists tightly together. No matter how tightly the rope is drawn or how hard the knots are tied, the magician is able to release himself almost instantly.

This escape is made possible by a very clever sleight executed by the magician as soon as he puts his hands behind his back. When the rope is tied around the right wrist, the knot should be on the inside of the wrist. When the magician puts his hands behind his back, he takes one of the ends of the rope in his left hand and makes a loop around the knot already tied. This loop is hidden at once by the back of the left wrist, and the wrists are then tied together. To escape, it is only necessary to pull the wrists apart. The loop will straighten out and leave ample room to withdraw the left hand, which can then untie the knot on the right wrist.

DISSOLVING KNOTS

THIS is an excellent and little known rope trick, which has been a favorite with some of the professional magicians. In effect, three overhand knots are tied in a piece of clothes rope or manila rope, as shown opposite. The ends of the rope are given to two spectators. Both pull, and presto! the knots dissolve away under their very eyes.

When the three knots have been tied, as shown, put the loops together, the right one on top of the center one, and these two on top of the left-hand loop. Take care not to turn any of the loops around. Put all three loops over the left hand. Pass the right-hand end of the rope between the first and second fingers of the left hand, and grip it tightly between these fingers.

Now grasp the loops with the right hand, and turn them so they are suspended over the left thumb. This simple movement causes the end held between the fingers to be passed right through the coils, and undoes the knots.

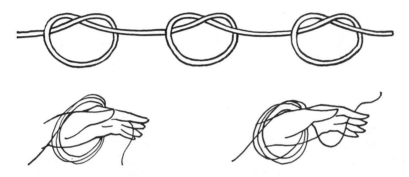

Give the left-hand end to one spectator, and the right-hand end to another. Tell them to pull, and the rope will come out straight, free from knots.

THE TWENTIETH-CENTURY ROPE TIE

This rope tie is frequently used by professsional magicians and by so-called "spirit" workers who are bound and placed in a cabinet and then free themselves to ring bells, rattle tambourines, and make other spirit manifestations.

The magician's hands are tied together behind his back, the rope passing around the wrists. There is no trick about the tying; it is perfectly fair and above aboard. A screen is placed in front of the magician and in a minute or two he steps out from behind it with the rope untied and his hands free.

The method of escape is illustrated on page 28. The magician passes his hands downward. When they are near his knees, he seats himself on a chair or on the floor, crosses his legs, and proceeds to draw first one foot and then the other out of the loop formed by his arms. He then brings his hands up to his mouth and loosens the knots with his teeth.

Clothes rope or sash cord is best to use, as it is more difficult to tie a tight knot in these materials than in ordinary rope. Another point is that the wrists should be tied near the heel of the hand, and not about the upper wrist. This will provide more room to work with.

THE CHAIR ROPE TIE

IN THIS trick the magician is securely tied in the position shown opposite, with a piece of rope. One end of the rope is tied around his right wrist, the free end of the rope is then brought under the seat of the chair and, after being drawn tight, is tied around the left wrist. A screen is then placed in front of him and, in a moment or two, he asks that it be removed. He is discovered seated on the chair in the same position as before, but with his coat off! The fact that it is impossible for him to touch one hand with the other and also impossible for him to untie and retie the rope so quickly makes the trick an exceptionally effective one.

The secret of this trick lies in the fact that in tying the second wrist the rope is drawn under the seat and is under a tension. In this condition it is not possible to tie a really firm knot on the second wrist. A little experimenting will show that this is so. The result is that, in the second knot, the end is simply tied around the rope, forming a sort of running knot.

When the screen is put in place, the magician spreads his knees and leans forward in the chair until he can bring his hands together,

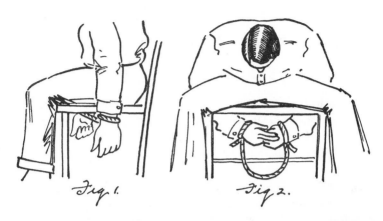

Fig. 1.   *Fig. 2.*

as in Fig. 2. He then pulls the knot on his left wrist. It will slide along the rope, enlarging the loop on the left wrist. This enables the magician to withdraw his left hand and remove his coat. The left hand is then put back in the loop, which is drawn tight, as though it were a slip-noose.

KNOTS, SPLICES, AND FANCY KNOT WORK

KNOTS

THE subject of Knots is a fascinating one and many people have devoted themselves to studying it as a hobby. Examples of each new knot they learn to make are tacked up on a display board, and an extremely interesting and unusual collection can be made in this way. Many of the knots in common use today were invented centuries ago and can be seen in old pictures and utilitarian and artistic objects. Thus the reef knot or square knot was widely used in ancient Greece and Rome and was used as a decoration on the handles of vases and for tying women's girdles. The Romans called it the Hercules knot and claimed that it had been invented by Hercules. Other knots known to the ancient Greeks included the clove hitch, running knot, lark's head, and jug sling. The carrick bend was one of the earliest knots known by the English people, and appeared in the coat of arms of Hereward the Wake, the warrior who defied William the Conqueror when he invaded England in 1066.

ELEMENTARY KNOTS

1. Half Hitch   2. Overhand Knot

1. The **Half Hitch** is sometimes used for temporarily making fast a line to a post or a spar. It is the basic part of many other knots.

2. The **Overhand Knot** is used only in making other knots; it is never used alone, as it does not hold fast.

3 Figure Eight   4. Stevedore's Knot

3. The **Figure-Eight Knot** is sometimes put on the end of a rope to prevent the end from slipping or unreeving through a block or eyebolt.

4. The **Stevedore's Knot** is used for the same purpose as the Figure-Eight knot.

KNOTS FOR JOINING TWO ROPES TOGETHER

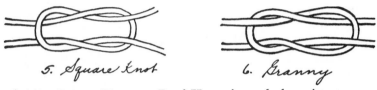

5. Square Knot   6. Granny

5. The **Square Knot**, or **Reef Knot**, is made by tying two overhand knots. The second overhand knot must be tied in the opposite way from the first, otherwise you will have a Granny Knot (Fig. 6) which will not hold fast. Practice tying the reef knot until you are sure you can get it right every time, as it is probably the most useful of all knots, while a granny is utterly worthless.

7. Surgeons' Knot

7. The **Surgeon's Knot** is made with double or triple overhand knots; it is sometimes used by surgeons when operating.

8. The **Sheet Bend, Weaver's Knot,** or **Becket Bend,** is a simple knot consisting of a bight or loop in one rope, and a half hitch in the other rope. It is useful to unite two ropes of different sizes, and it is also the knot used in netting. It is tied by crossing one rope end (1) across rope end 2 as in Fig. 8a, bringing the end of rope 1 down around rope 2, as shown by the dotted line, and then up as in Fig. 8b. The end of rope 1 is then passed behind the standing

part of rope 2 and down through the bight or loop that has been formed in rope 2 (Fig. 8c).

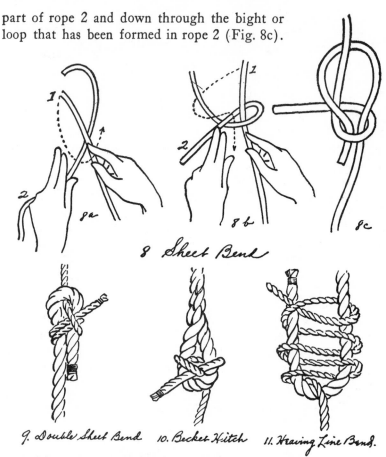

8 Sheet Bend

9. Double Sheet Bend   10. Becket Hitch   11. Heaving Line Bend.

9. The **Double Sheet** Bend is more secure than a single bend, particularly when fastening a small rope to a much larger one.

10. The **Becket Hitch** is exactly like the sheet bend except that it is used to fasten or hitch a rope to a becket or eye, instead of to fasten two ropes together.

11. The **Heaving Line Bend** is used to bend or fasten a small rope to a larger one. When mooring a ship, one end of a light heaving line is first thrown to a person on shore and the opposite end is then attached to a hawser, which the people on shore draw to them by means of the heaving line.

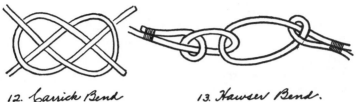

12. Carrick Bend   13. Hawser Bend.

12. The **Carrick Bend** is frequently used to bend large hawsers together. It does not jam as hard as a Sheet Bend or Reef Knot when tension is applied to the ends of the two ropes.

13. The **Hawser Bend**, or **Half Hitch**, and **Seizing Bend** is used to join two hawsers or other ropes which must pass through a small opening. It takes up less space than the carrick bend. Seizing is a round lashing used to hold two ropes or two parts of a single rope together, and is described below.

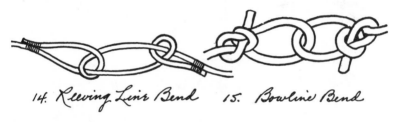

14. Reeving Line Bend   15. Bowline Bend

14. The **Reeving Line Bend** is very similar to the Hawser Bend and is used for the same purposes.

15. The **Bowline Bend** is a very secure method of bending two lines together and can be used whenever absolute safety is required. The Bowline Knot is described below under "Knots Used to Make a Loop or a Noose."

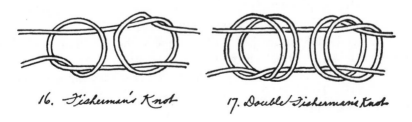

16. Fisherman's Knot   17. Double Fisherman's Knot

16. The **Fisherman's Knot**, or **Englishman's Knot**, is chiefly used for fastening pieces of gut which sometimes slip when joined by a Reef Knot or Sheet Bend. It consists of two overhand knots, each formed over the standing part of the other piece of gut or line.

17. The **Double Fisherman's Knot** is similar to the single knot, but is a little stronger.

KNOTS FOR SECURING ROPES TO RINGS OR SPARS

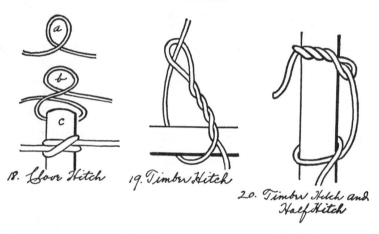

18. Clove Hitch   19. Timber Hitch

20. Timber Hitch and Half Hitch

18. The **Clove Hitch** is one of the most commonly used knots for fastening a boat's painter to a post or mooring pile, and also has many other uses. It is usually made by throwing a half hitch over the post and then, with the free end, throwing another half hitch over the first one.

19. The **Timber Hitch** is used for towing spars or for securing a rope quickly, though usually temporarily, to a spar or other object. The twists should follow the lay of the rope or the direction in which the strands of the rope are twisted.

20. The **Timber Hitch and Half Hitch** is used for the same purposes as the Timber Hitch; the Half Hitch keeps a towed spar pointed fore and aft.

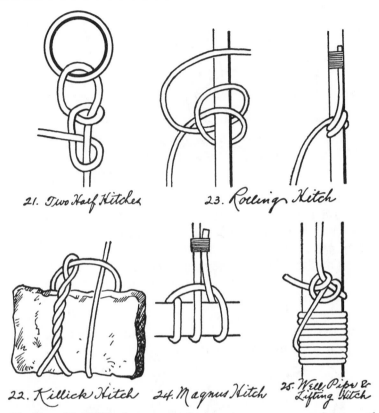

21. Two Half Hitches   23. Rolling Hitch

22. Killick Hitch   24. Magnus Hitch   25. Well-Pipe & Lifting Hitch

21. **Two Half Hitches** are used to secure a rope to a ring or other object, usually for a temporary period.

22. The **Killick Hitch** is the same as the Timber Hitch and Half Hitch, except that the Half Hitch is made in the opposite direction. It is good for lifting boards, spars, or rocks.

23. The **Rolling Hitch** is used to take the strain off one rope by means of another rope or to fasten a rope to a spar when the tension is to be applied parallel to the axis of the spar.

24. The **Magnus Hitch** is quite similar to the Rolling Hitch, but the free end of the rope is seized to the standing part.

25. The **Lifting** or **Well-Pipe Hitch** is used by circus roustabouts to secure the guy ropes of the "big top" to stakes driven into the ground.

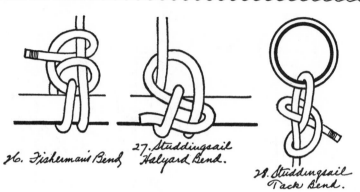

26. *Fisherman's Bend*

27. *Studdingsail Halyard Bend.*

28. *Studdingsail Tack Bend.*

26. The **Fisherman's Bend**, or **Anchor Bend**, is an easily made and exceptionally strong knot. The end of the rope can be secured with a Half Hitch or can be stopped down or seized against the standing part.

27. The **Studdingsail Halyard Bend** is an excellent knot which does not easily come adrift; the harder the pull, the more tightly the knot is jammed.

28. The **Studdingsail Tack Bend**, or **Topsail Sheet Bend**, is another useful bend which will not come adrift when the strain on the rope is temporarily relaxed.

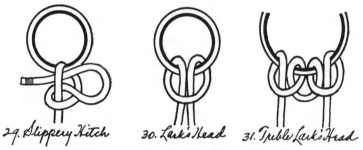

29. *Slippery Hitch*   30. *Lark's Head*   31. *Treble Lark's Head*

29. The **Slippery Hitch** is useful for securing a line, such as the painter of a small boat, to a ring. It can be undone in a jiffy by pulling on the free end of the rope.

30. The **Lark's Head** is used for securing a rope to a ring when there is to be tension on both standing parts. It is made by doubling the rope in the center and then passing the two ends through the loop.

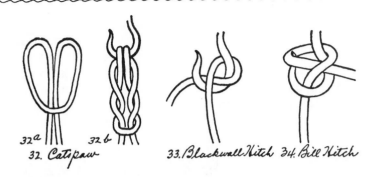

32ᵃ 32ᵇ
32. Catspaw   33. Blackwall Hitch 34. Bill Hitch

31. The **Treble Lark's Head** is used as an ornamental knot, and is sometimes used by sailors to cover rings, a number of the knots being tied around a ring until it is covered.

32. The **Catspaw** is used for securing a rope to a hook. Fig. 32a shows the first step in the formation of the knot. The two bights or loops are twisted in opposite directions and then hung over the hook. The completed hitch is shown in Fig. 32b.

33. The **Blackwall Hitch** is used for the same purpose as the Catspaw. It is not a secure knot and should not be used when a heavy weight is to be lifted or where safety depends upon the knot holding firmly. It is chiefly used when a rope is put on the stretch for some purpose.

34. The **Bill Hitch** is another knot sometimes used to secure a rope to a hook.

KNOTS USED TO MAKE A LOOP OR A NOOSE

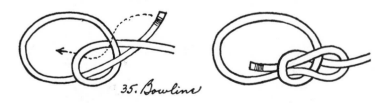

35. Bowline

35. The **Bowline** is one of the most important of all knots and is sometimes called "the king of knots." It will never slip or jam and

it can be cast loose at once when the tension is slackened. It is tied in exactly the same way that the Sheet Bend is tied (See Figs. 8a, 8b, and 8c). Put the end of the rope across the standing part of the same rope; bring the end down to the left and under the standing part, at the same time forming the little loop or bight in the standing part. Then pass the end around the standing part and down through the bight.

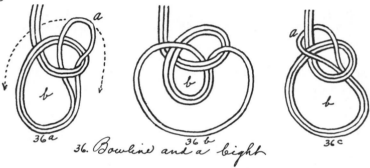

36. *Bowline and a bight*

36. The **Bowline on a Bight** is made in the center, or bight, of a doubled rope; it is frequently used by sailors to sling a man over the side. Fig. 36a shows the first step in tying it. Next pass the small bight A down and completely around and over the large bight B, as in Fig. 36b. Then bring bight A up on the other side of the knot to the position shown in Fig. 36c.

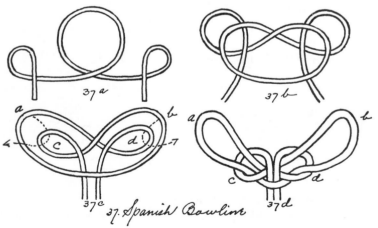

37. *Spanish Bowline*

37. The **Spanish Bowline** is an interesting variation of the regular bowline. Form three loops as in Fig. 37a, and turn the center loop down as in Fig. 37b. Enlarge the center loop until it surrounds the two smaller loops (Fig. 37c). Then push the bights A and B up through the small loops C and D to complete the knot.

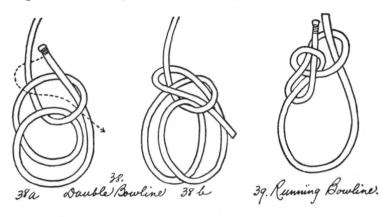

38a   *Double Bowline*   38b   39. *Running Bowline.*

38. The **Double Bowline** is frequently used as a sling because it has two ropes in the main bight which makes it more comfortable to sit in. Its formation is made clear in Figs 38a and 38b.

39. The **Running Bowline** is a bowline made around the standing part of a rope; it is probably the best temporary running knot or slip knot. It is made by tying a regular bowline around the standing part.

40a   40b   40. *Slip Knot*   41. *Crabber's Eye Knot*

40. The **Slip Knot, Slip Noose,** or **Running Knot,** is a temporary running knot useful for many purposes, including tying up packages. To tie it, form a loop as in Fig. 40a, put your hand through the loop, grasp the standing part at A, and draw the standing part back through the loop.

41. The **Crabber's Eye Knot,** or **Crossed Running Knot,** is a variation of the ordinary running knot.

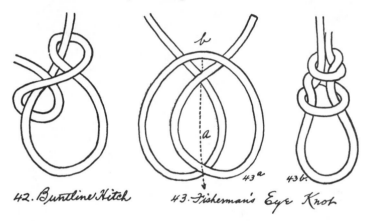

42. *Buntline Hitch*   43. *Fisherman's Eye Knot*

42. The **Buntline Hitch** is a running knot that was formerly used to secure the buntlines to the sails. The knot holds tight as long as tension is applied, since the end of the rope is jammed into place.

43. The **Fisherman's Eye Knot,** or **True Lovers' Knot,** is chiefly

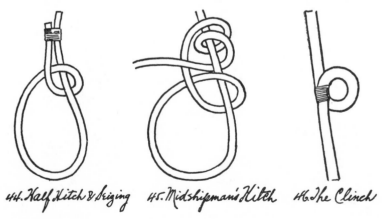

44. *Half Hitch & Siezing*   45. *Midshipman's Hitch*   46. *The Clinch*

used by fishermen to make a loop in a piece of gut. It will not easily slip, but it is a hard knot to untie. To make it, form two loops as in Fig. 43a, put your hand through the loops at A, grasp the rope at B, and pull B back through A. This forms two overhand knots which jam against each other when you pull on the loop.

44. The Half Hitch and Seizing is one of the simplest methods of making a loop in the end of a line.

45. The **Midshipman's Hitch** is a good running knot which jams down tightly against an object in the loop as long as tension is applied and is easily cast loose when the tension is slackened.

46. The **Clinch** is made by forming a small loop and seizing the parts together. It is used in making the two following clinches and is sometimes used by sailors to keep a rope from running through a block.

47. The **Outside Clinch** serves as a running knot and is made by passing the standing part of the rope through a simple clinch.

48. The **Inside Clinch** is a better knot in some respects than the Outside Clinch, since it jams on itself when passed around a spar or other object.

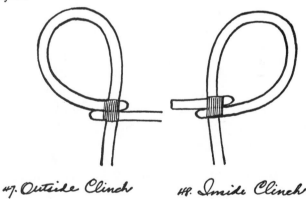

47. Outside Clinch   48. Inside Clinch

49. The **Hackamore, Jar Sling,** or **Jug Sling,** can be used to carry a jar or jug, the neck of the jug being placed through the center of the knot and the projecting loop and the two free rope ends being used for carrying. It is made by forming two loops as in Fig. 49a,

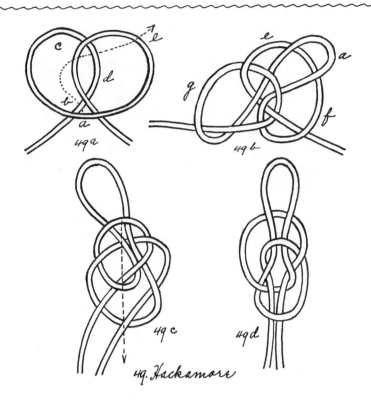

49. *Hackamore*

and then bringing the part marked A under B, over C, under D, and over E, when the knot will appear as in Fig. 49b. Turn the loop E-F back and under loop G, so that both ends of the rope come out of the knot together as in Fig 49c. Turn the loop G down to the position shown in Fig. 49d, and the knot will be tied.

50. The **Masthead Knot**, or **Jury Knot**, was formerly used to place over the head of a jury mast (one rigged to replace a broken mast). Stays were bent to the three bights, and one of the free ends also could serve as a stay. To make the knot, form three loops as in Fig. 50a. Pull part C under B and over A; then pull D over E and under F. Put the center loop over a post or hook or take it in your teeth and pull the knot into the shape shown in Fig. 50b.

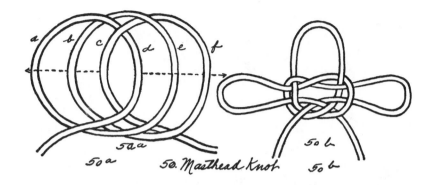

50. Masthead Knot

51. The **Tomfool Knot** may be used as a jar sling or as a pair of rope handcuffs. To tie it, make two loops as shown in Fig. 51a. Pull part B under A, and pull C over D. This will complete the knot as in Fig. 51b.

52. The **Shamrock Knot**, or **Japanese Masthead Knot**, is one of the most ornamental knots, and can be used as a jar sling. To tie it, make two interlocking overhand knots as in Fig. 52a. Pull A to the left between B and C, and pull D to the right between E and F.

53. The **Artillery Knot**, or **Man-Harness**, is used by soldiers when several men have to pull a piece of artillery or some other heavy object by a single rope. A knot is made in the rope for each man to pass his arm and shoulder through. To tie the knot, make a loop as in Fig. 53a, and turn the loop down over the standing part as in Fig. 53b. Then pull part A up under B and over C (Fig. 53c). When the knot is pulled tight, it appears as in Fig. 53d.

KNOTS USED FOR SHORTENING A ROPE

54. The **Sheepbank** was used by sailors long ago, but has not been employed for many years. It was used to shorten a rope temporarily and also to lessen the strain on a weakened rope, the weakened part being placed in the center of the knot. It is made by arranging the rope as in Fig. 54a, and then making Half Hitches with the ends over the looped standing part (Fig. 54b). If the ends are free, they can

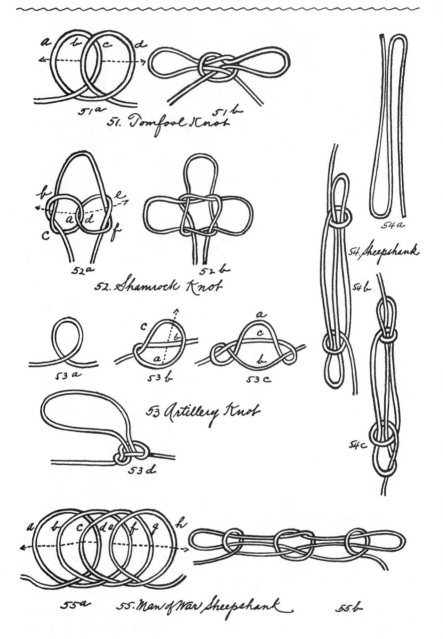

51. Tomfool Knot

52. Shamrock Knot

53 Artillery Knot

54. Sheepshank

55. Man of War Sheepshank

be passed through the end bights as in Fig. 54c to make the knot considerably more secure.

55. The **Man-of-War Sheepshank**, or **Knotted Sheepshank**, is no longer used, but is an interesting knot to make. Form four loops as in Fig. 55a. Reach under A and B and over C with the left hand, and grasp D. Reach over H and G and under F with the right hand, and grasp E. Pull the hands apart and the knot will appear as shown in Fig. 55b.

56. The **Overhand Knot** for shortening a sling is shown in Fig. 56. To make it, form a loop in the end of the sling as in Fig. 56a. Turn the loop up and over the two standing parts as in Fig. 56b. Hold parts A and B together in one hand and pass them behind part C.

ORNAMENTAL AND OTHER KNOTS

57. The **Three-Strand Turk's Head** is started by arranging the rope as in Fig. 57a. The center A is placed over a rod, rope, or other object, and the parts arranged as in Fig. 57b. The ends are then passed around the knot following the original arrangement or lay of the parts until each part is trebled as in Fig. 57c.

If it is not possible to slip the rope arranged as in Fig. 57a over the end of the object on which the Turk's Head is to be made, the knot should be formed as shown in Figs. 57d to 57i. Pass the rope around the object three times. The end A is the one with which the knot is to be worked. Bring C down over B (Fig. 57e), and bring A up over C and under B (Fig. 57f). Pass A down over C and under B (Fig. 57g). Then bring C down over B again (Fig. 57h) and bring the end A up over C and under B (Fig. 57i). These movements are then repeated until the knot is finished.

58. The **Four-Strand Turk's Head** is made as follows: Pass the end A (Fig. 58a) under C, over D, and under B. This gives the arrangement shown in Fig. 58b. Next pass the end A under E, over F and G and under H. The rope will then appear as in Fig. 58c. Pass the end A over B, under I, over J, under K, over L, under M, and over N. This gives Fig. 58d. Place the center X over a rope or

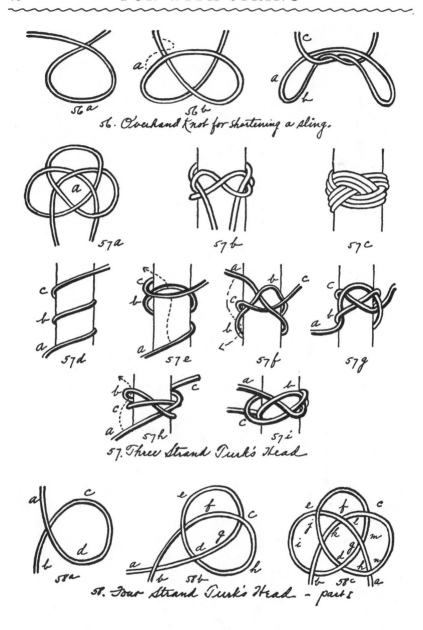

56. Overhand Knot for shortening a sling.

57. Three Strand Turk's Head

58. Four Strand Turk's Head - parts

rod and arrange the parts of the rope as in Fig. 58e. Then pass one of the ends around the knot, following the original arrangement or lay of the rope until all the parts are trebled.

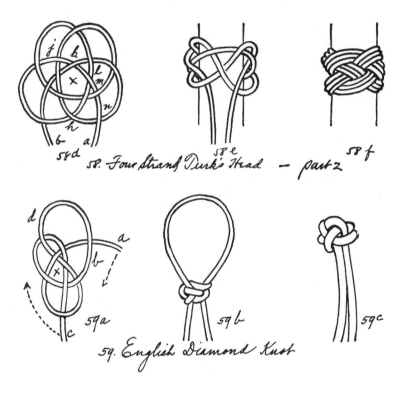

58d   58. Four Strand Turk's Head — part 2   58f

59a   59b   59c

59. English Diamond Knot

59. The **English Diamond Knot** is used by sailors to ornament their knife or other lanyards. To tie it, the rope or cord is arranged as in Fig. 59a. Pass the end A under and over part B and down through the center at X. Pass the end C around and under part D and then down through the center at X. When the knot is drawn tight, it will appear as in Fig. 59b. If the loop is drawn all the way down, the knot will appear as in Fig. 59c, a form suitable for decorating the looped end of a lanyard.

60. The **Monkey's Fist** is used by sailors to weight the end of a heaving line and is also sometimes used as an ornamental knot. To

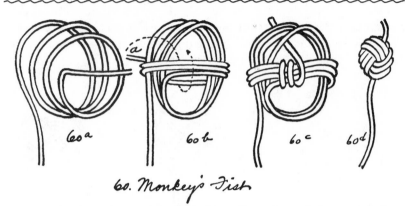

60. Monkey's Fist

tie it, make three loops as in Fig. 60a. Pass the end A around these
loops three times as in Fig. 60b. Then pass the end A through
the center of the first loops as shown by the dotted line, and three
times around the second set of loops (Fig. 60c). Draw all the loops
tight and the completed knot will appear as in Fig. 60d.

61. Crown Knot

61. The **Crown Knot** is used on the ends of ropes to keep the
strands from untwisting or fraying. It is generally combined with a
back splice, each strand being tucked over and under the strands in
the standing part. To make a Crown Knot, unlay the strands for a
short distance from the end as in Fig. 61a. Form a bight or loop with
one of the strands, and pass the end of the next strand through this
bight (Fig. 61b). Then pass the end of the third strand down through
the bight of the second strand, and the end of the first strand down
through the bight of the third. Pull the strands tight and the knot
will appear as in Fig. 61c. The ends may be cut off short or back
spliced into the standing part.

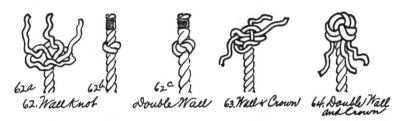

62ᵃ 62ᵇ 62ᶜ
62. Wall Knot   Double Wall 63. Wall & Crown 64. Double Wall and Crown

62. The **Wall Knot** is made in the same way as the Crown Knot, but each strand is passed up (instead of down) through the bight of the strand next to it. The ends are usually whipped as in Fig. 62b. A Double Wall Knot (Fig. 62c) is frequently used to keep the strands of a rope from untwisting or unreeving. First make a wall knot, but before pulling it tight, pass each strand again through the bight of the strand next to it.

63. The **Wall and Crown Knot**, as its name implies, is a wall knot with a crown on top of it. In the old days it was used for the cat-o'-nine tails.

64. The **Double Wall and Crown** or **Man-rope Knot** is used on the ends of manropes to furnish a hold for a man who has fallen overboard. First make a wall and crown knot, but before tightening the strands, follow around the wall knot with each strand, and then around the crown knot with each strand. Pull the knot tight and cut the ends off close.

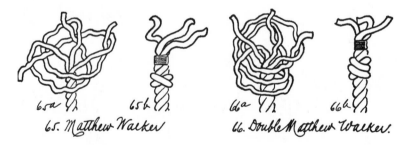

65ᵃ 65ᵇ
65. Matthew Walker   66ᵃ 66ᵇ
66. Double Matthew Walker.

65. The **Matthew Walker Knot** is very similar to the wall knot, but each strand is passed upward through the bights of the next two strands (Fig. 65a). The best way to make it is first to make a wall knot and then, one after the other, pass the end of each strand up through the bight of one more strand.

66. The **Double Matthew Walker Knot** is formed by first making a single Matthew Walker Knot, and then passing each strand up through an additional bight which, in this case, will be its own bight.

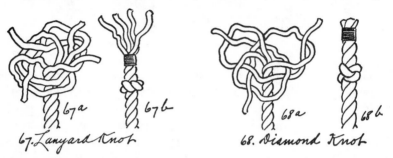

67. Lanyard Knot   68. Diamond Knot

67. The **Lanyard Knot** is a Matthew Walker Knot made with four-strand rope. Each strand is passed up through the bights of the next two strands (Fig. 67a). Its name is derived from the fact that it was used by sailors to keep certain ropes known as lanyards from slipping through the deadeyes through which they were passed.

68. The **Diamond Knot** is similar to the Wall Knot, but each strand is passed up through the bight of the next strand but one, or the second strand away (Fig. 68a). The best way to make it is to make a wall knot and then remove each strand from its bight and pass it up through the bight of the succeeding strand.

WHIPPING AND SEIZING

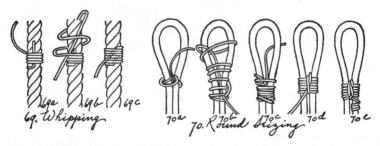

69. Whipping   70. Round Seizing

69. **A Whipping** is a lashing made around the end of a rope to keep the strands from untwisting or fraying. Figs. 69a, 69b, and 69c show the method in most common use among sailors. The cord or

twine used for the whipping should always be wound around the rope against the lay of the rope; that is, in the opposite direction to that in which the strands of the rope are twisted. The last three or four turns are wound around the free end of the cord, which is then pulled tight and cut off close.

70. A Seizing is a small lashing for holding two ropes, or two parts of the same rope, together. The Round Seizing, which is used to form an eye in a rope, is shown in Figs. 70a to 70e. A small eye is spliced in the cord being used for the seizing, and the end of the cord is passed around both parts of the rope and up through the eye (Fig. 70a). The cord is then wound around both ropes eight or ten times, and the end is brought back down and through the eye (Fig. 70b). Each turn is pulled tight, and a second series of turns, called riding turns, are made. The end of the cord is then passed between the upper two turns of the first or inner series of turns (Fig. 70c). Two "frapping turns" are then passed around the seizing from top to bottom (Fig. 70d) and are secured with a clove hitch (Fig. 70e). The free end of the cord is then wound around one of the ropes several times and secured with two Half Hitches.

When only one series of turns is made around the ropes, it is called a Flat Seizing.

A Racking Seizing is made by passing the turns figure-eight fashion (Fig. 70f) instead of passing them around the outside of the ropes only. It is finished off with frapping turns in the same manner as the Round Seizing. A Racking Seizing is used when tension is to be applied only to one rope or part, instead of equally to both ropes or parts.

70f
Racking
Seizing.

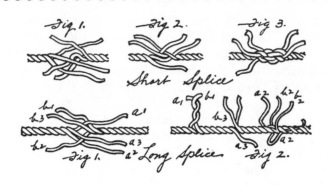

SPLICING

SPLICING is a method of permanently joining the ends of two ropes or of bending a rope back on itself to form an eye or loop. If properly done, splicing does not weaken a rope. There are two kinds of splice used to join two ropes together, the short splice and the long splice.

To make a **short splice,** the ends of both ropes are unlaid for about a foot and the strands are interlaid or married as in Fig. 1. Beginning with any one strand, it is tucked against the lay of the rope (or the direction in which the strands of the rope are twisted) over one and under one strand of the opposite rope (Fig. 2). A marlinespike or other pointed instrument is used to open the lay of the rope for the strands to be pushed through. The operation is repeated with the two remaining strands. The strands of the second rope are then tucked into the first rope, passing over one and under one strand, as before (Fig. 3). Each strand is then tucked twice more and the ends are cut off close.

For a **tapered splice** which will pass more easily over a sheave or other object, cut away threads from each strand after the first tuck so that each strand is two-thirds its original size. After the second tuck, the strands are cut away until they are one-third their original size.

For a **long splice** the ends of the two ropes are unlaid farther than for a short splice and are then interlaid in the same manner. The procedure from then on, however, is different and is as follows:

A strand of one rope, as a1, in Fig. 1, is unlaid for quite a distance, and the corresponding strand of the other rope, b1, is laid in the opening left by a1. The remaining ends of each rope are twisted up together for convenience, the ropes are turned end for end, and the first operation is repeated with two other corresponding strands, as a2 and b2. The remaining strands of each rope, a3 and b3, are left in their original positions. This leaves pairs of strands at three positions as in Fig. 2. Each of these strands is halved. Then two of the halves at each position, as of a2 and b2, Fig. 2, are tied together with an overhand knot, and the remaining halves are tucked over one and under one of the full remaining strands of the rope. After all strands have been tucked, the loose ends are trimmed off smooth.

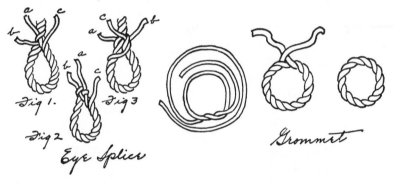

An **eye splice** is made by the same method as that employed for making a short splice, except that the rope is first brought back upon itself to form the desired size of eye, and the strands are then tucked into the standing part of the rope. Figs. 1, 2, and 3 make the formation of the splice clear.

A **grommet** is a ring made by joining the two ends of a piece of rope by means of a short or long splice. It can also be made from a single strand of rope. The strand should be somewhat more than three times as long as the circumference of the grommet. Lay up the strand in the form of a circle, as shown above, twisting it around itself. When the two ends come together, cut each one down to half its original diameter, tie them together with an overhand knot, and tuck them under as in a long splice. Grommets can be used for playing ring toss or for the handles of chests.

SQUARE-KNOT WORK

SQUARE-KNOT work, like netting, has for many years been a favorite diversion of sailors, who use it to make many beautiful articles during their watches below on long sea voyages. Many of the sailors in the United States Navy of today—despite its modernity —are skilful exponents of this fascinating craft, which has been handed down to them by the shellbacks of the old China trade windjammers. Some believe that square-knot work originated many centuries ago in Arabia, and it is said that the men who sailed with Columbus bartered articles made by square-knotting with the Indians whom they encountered in America.

The elementary principles of square-knot work can best be learned by making some of the simpler articles such as lanyards for a knife or whistle, or for use as a dog leash, belts, and shade pulls. When the method employed in doing square-knot work has been mastered by this means, square-knot handbags and centerpieces can be made. These are truly beautiful pieces of work and their making will provide one with a worth-while and life-long hobby or avocation.

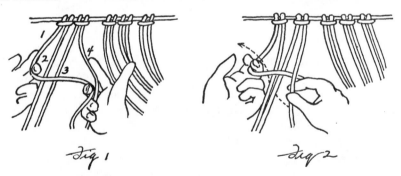

Fig. 1   Fig. 2

Figures 1 to 6 show how the cords used in square-knot work are arranged, and how the knots are tied.

To practice, double and loop several pieces of cord over a curtain-rod or a piece of dowel, as shown in Fig. 1. (If you were going to make a belt, the cords would be looped across the bar of the belt buckle.)

Four strands, such as the four strands on the left in Fig. 1, are generally used as the basis for square-knot work. Start your practice work, therefore, by pairing off the cords in sets of four.

To start the knotting, take the two center strands (2 and 3, Fig. 1), and fasten their ends to some stationary object or to a tension hook (described later), so they will be stretched out tight. Then take the left-hand strand in the left hand, as shown. With the right hand, draw it across the two center strands. Hold it between the right-hand fingers, as in Fig 1. Take the right-hand strand between the right thumb and forefinger; and bring it down over the left-hand strand (Fig. 2).

Now pass the right-hand strand to the left, *under* the two center strands. Bring the end out through the loop *a*, Fig. 2. This makes Fig. 3. Pull the strands up quite tightly. This completes the first half of one square knot.

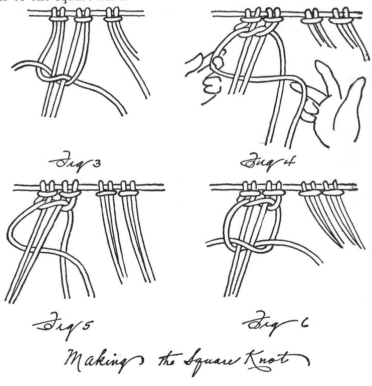

Fig 3

Fig 4

Fig 5

Fig 6

Making the Square Knot

To finish the knot, pass the left-hand strand *under* the two center strands (Fig. 4). Bring the right-hand strand down *under* the left-hand strand (Fig. 5), then pass the right-hand strand to the left, *over* the two center strands. Pass the end down through the loop *a,* Fig. 5. This makes Fig. 6. Pull the strands up tight and the second half of the knot will be completed.

The whole operation really consists of tying a regular square knot around the two central cords.

Making Successive Rows

In square-knot work, as has already been explained, four strands are used for each knot. The first row of knots in a belt or other article is made by repeating the knotting process illustrated in Figs. 1 to 6 right across the row. When you start the second row, make the first knot with strands 3 and 4 of the first or left-hand set of four strands, and strands 1 and 2 of the second set of four strands (Fig. 7). Continue across the row in the same manner.

The third row is made with the same strands as those used in the first row; the fourth row is made with the same strands as those used in the second row, and so on.

Pointing Square-Knot Work

Square-knot work is frequently brought to a point at the center, or to points at each side, in order to vary the design.

To bring the work to a point at the center (Fig. 8), drop two strands on each side of each row of knots until the four center strands come to a point.

To make points on each side of the work (Fig. 9), drop two strands from the center on each side of each row of knots.

To make a point on one side only, drop two strands from the opposite side of each row of knots.

After a point in the center has been made, and you wish to bring the work down even with the point on each side, start at the outside on each side and pick up two strands on each side of each row of knots (See Fig. 10).

Fig. 7   *Fig. 8*   *Fig. 9*

After points have been made on each side and you wish to bring the center of the work down even with the points, start in the center and pick up two strands on each side of each row of knots.

If a point has been made on one side and you wish to bring the opposite side down even with the point, start at the outside on the opposite side and pick up two strands on each row of knots.

Flats

Fig. 12 illustrates what are known in square-knot work as *flats*. They are made by repeating the knot shown in Figs. 1 to 6; that is, by repeating a square knot around two central strands.

Spiral Formations

A variation of the regular knotting shown in Figs. 1 to 6 is produced by making a series of half knots, one after the other, around the two central strands. This makes a spiral strand. By repeating the first half of the square knot, a spiral twisting to the right is produced. If the second half of the square knot is repeated, the spiral will twist to the left.

Open Mesh Work

Open mesh work is sometimes used in making square-knot handbags. It is illustrated in Fig. 13. Assume that each mesh is to be one-half inch in length. To make the mesh work, space the first half of the square knot, as at *a* in Fig. 13, one-half inch below the last row of square knots. Then tie the second half of the knot tightly against the first part.

In order to make all the meshes the same length, it is best to cut a thin stick shaped like a ruler, with a width equal to the distance that the first row of knots in the mesh work is to be spaced from the last row of knots. The stick is inserted between the two center strands when tying each knot, and the knots are tied against its lower edge.

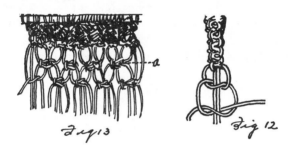

Fig. 13   *Fig. 12*

Half-Hitch Work

An interesting variation of pattern is obtained in square-knot handbags, belts, or fabrics by introducing half-hitch work, as well as open mesh work. Fig. 14 shows how slanting rows of half hitches are worked into a background of square-knot work.

Half-hitch work is executed by holding a single strand (No. 1) tight, and making half hitches around it with another strand (No. 2). Make the hitches by passing strand No. 2 under strand No. 1, leaving a loop; then put the end of strand No. 2 over strand No. 1 and down through the loop. This operation is repeated until the line or row of half hitches is the desired length.

Rows of half hitches can be made slanting to the right, slanting to the left, straight across, and straight up and down. To make a row slanting to the right, take the strand that is to be the No. 1 strand and hold it out tight at a 45-degree angle with the right hand. Then make the half hitches around it with the left hand. A row slant-

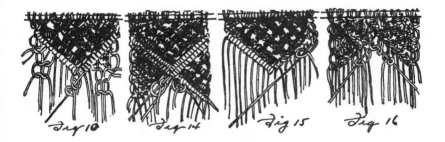

ing to the left is made in the same way, except that the No. 1 strand is held out to the left by the left hand.

To make a row of half hitches straight across a piece of solid square-knot work, the last or bottom row of square knots must run evenly across the piece. Take the left hand outside cord and make two half hitches around it with each of the down-hanging cords. Carry the cord right across until it becomes the right-hand outside cord. If preferable, the original right-hand cord may be carried across, instead of the left-hand one. Draw the half hitches up tight for, if this is not done, the row of half hitches will be wider than the other rows. To keep the row the proper width, it may be necessary to make only one half hitch (instead of two) with every second or third down-hanging cord.

When a piece of square-knot work is brought to a point in the center and a slanting row of half hitches is to be made on each side of the point, bring the outside strand from one side to the center, and make two half hitches around it with each down-hanging cord (Fig. 15). Then bring the outside strand from the other side to the center and make two half hitches around it with each down-hanging cord, including the cord that was brought to the center from the opposite side (Fig. 10).

When several slanting rows of half hitches are to be made, alternate the outside cords. First use the outside cord on the left, for example, then the outside cord on the right, then the left, and then the right. Each time except the first, make a half hitch with the outside cord previously brought to the center.

Fig. 16 shows how slanting rows of half hitches that come from the center to each side are made. Each side is first worked to a point. Then the two central strands are picked out and tied in an overhand knot. The two central strands are then extended at a 45-degree angle to left and right, and two half hitches are made around them with the down-hanging cords. It is necessary to knot the two central cords, since otherwise there would be an opening between the rows of half hitches.

Additional designs that can be made by using the types of half-hitch work described above include diamonds, X-shaped crosses, and diagonal rows of half-hitch work extending all the way across the piece.

Length of Strands

The working strands used in square-knot work should be at least 3½ times the length of the article that is being made.

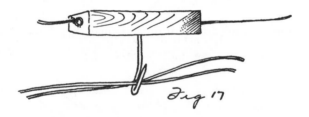

Tension Hooks For Square-Knot Work

Old hands at square-knot work use a tension hook of the type shown in Fig. 17. The hook is screwed into a block of 1-inch wood; and cords are attached to screw-eyes in each end of the block. The cords are tied around the waist of the person doing the work. One end of the square-knot work is attached to a dowel or rod, as already explained. The two central cords around which square knots are being tied are knotted and looped over the hook. By moving backward or forward, the right amount of tension is placed on the central cords.

SQUARE-KNOT BELTS

A BELT is one of the easiest and most satisfactory articles with which to start your square-knot work. All the variations in design that have been described can be used. Solid square-knot work can be alternated with open mesh work; and diamonds and X-shaped crosses of half-hitch work can be incorporated in the pattern. Six-thread, nine-thread, twelve-thread or fifteen-thread seine twine can be used satisfactorily, or the belts can be made of No. 3 mercerized cotton or silk cord.

You will need a buckle for your belt, and this can be purchased at a department store or ten-cent store. Cut the strands of cord seven times the length of the belt you are going to make. Double the strands of cord in the middle and loop them on the bar of the buckle. The strands will then be 3½ times the length of the belt, which is the correct ratio.

The number of strands will depend upon the material used and the width of the buckle. The strands should be close together, and their number should be a multiple of four, since they must be paired off in groups of four for knotting. When they have been looped over the buckle, catch the buckle over a hook driven into the wall, or secure it in some other way so it will be stationary and you can pull against it to get the needed tension on the central cords around which the square knots are to be tied.

The simplest type of belt to make is one made throughout of solid square knot work. Such a belt is best finished off by bringing the strands to a point in the center and then making two or three slanting rows of half hitches on each side. When this has been done, soak the half hitches in water. This swells the fibers and causes the hitches to "set." Then cut off the loose ends of the strands close to the outer row of half hitches. No hole need be made for the tongue of the buckle, as it can be slipped into one of the spaces already in the fabric of the belt.

A belt loop to hold the pointed end of the belt in place after it has been buckled can be made by forming a three-strand Turk's Head around the body of the belt. (See page 45 for description of how to make a Turk's Head.)

After you have made a belt of square-knot work, you will be familiar with the work and can then go on to introduce open-mesh work and designs worked in half hitches.

SQUARE-KNOT SHADE PULLS

Interesting and decorative shade pulls for the window-shades in your own room can be made by square knotting, and ornamental cords of this description may also be used for dog leashes, whistle lanyards, or any other similar purposes.

The shade pull illustrated above is made by alternating a series of "flats" with right- and left-hand spiral formations. Flats, it will be remembered, are made by repeating a square knot around two or more central strands. A right-hand spiral is made by repeating the first half of the square knot a number of times, and a left-hand spiral is made by repeating the second half of the square knot.

To start a shade pull, take two lengths of cord (Dreadnaught Cord, size No. 120 is recommended), each 2 yards long. Double each cord, and put the looped ends over a hook driven into the wall. You will now have four cords, each 1 yard long, side by side. These are the central strands, or the core of the shade pull. If you are using a tension hook, fasten the four free ends to it.

The knotting work is done with another cord, which should be about 3 yards long. Tie it around the core with a square knot about 2 inches from the hook in the wall. Then make 20 to 25 square knots, one after the other, around the core. Continue by making about 15 half knots, using the first half of the square knot. This gives a right-hand spiral.

Next make 18 or 20 complete knots, and then 16 more half knots, using the second half of the square knot to give a left-hand spiral. Finish with 20 complete knots.

To make the tassel, knot the ends of all the cords together a number of times, until they form a round knot or ball. Then cut 50 lengths of cord, each 6 inches long. Lay these evenly on a table. Place the knob at the end of the pull in the middle of these cords, midway between the ends of the cords. Gather the short cords around the knot and tie a string around them. Arrange the cords around the knot until the knot is evenly covered. Then turn the upper ends of the cords down and bind them just below the knot, as shown in Fig. 18. Finish by cutting the cords off evenly.

SQUARE-KNOT NECKTIES

GOOD-LOOKING square-knot neckties can be made in one, two, or more colors. In this description, a two-color tie is described, which makes clear the method of arranging the strands to introduce different colors. Ties are generally made of crochet silk.

An attractive coloring is blue with a narrow edging of white and a white stripe down the center. It is made of 20 strands of blue and 8 strands of white, each 10 feet in length. The strands are grouped from left to right as follows: 2 white, 10 blue, 4 white, 10 blue, 2 white. Tie the strands to a rod or dowel in the order given.

Start the knotting at the center point of the strands, as described above. Use strands 1, 2, 3 and 4 (the first four on the left) for the first square knot, and use strands 5, 6, 7, and 8 for the second square knot. Continue across, using successive groups of 4 strands, until you reach the last 4 strands from which the last square knot in the first row is to be made. In tying this knot, reverse the usual procedure. Tie the second half first, and the first half last. This must be done to keep the colors in balance.

Start the second row of the knots by using strands 3, 4, 5 and 6 for the first square knot. In this row, reverse the *fourth* square knot, but not the last one.

Continue making rows of square knots, alternating them as above, until you have 30 rows. Pull each knot tight to make this part of the necktie firm.

After the thirtieth row, continue as before, but do not pull the knots tight, and gradually increase the distance between each row until there is a space of one-eighth inch between the knots. This makes this part of the necktie wider and makes it pliable so it can be easily tied. Continue tying the open work until the necktie is 20 inches long from the starting-point.

Finish the end by bringing the work to a point in the center and making three slanting rows of half hitches on each side of the point.

Now turn the work end for end and make solid square-knot work for a distance of 10 inches. Continue with the loose open work and make this end 12 inches long. Finish it off with a point and half hitches in the same manner as the opposite end.

A SQUARE-KNOT CENTERPIECE

This centerpiece, which is not difficult to make, is shown in Fig. 20. It can be made of crochet silk, mercerized crochet cotton or 9-thread seine twine.

First, make a ring of cord about one-half inch in diameter for the center. Then cut off 32 strands. Each strand should be six times the width of the centerpiece from the center to the edge. Thus, if the centerpiece is to be 12 inches wide, the distance from the center to the edge would be 6 inches, and each strand would be 36 inches long. A centerpiece may be started with any number of strands from 20 to 36. In this description, it is assumed that the beginning is made with 32 strands.

Double the strands in the middle and loop them over the center ring. Then pair them off in groups of four, as in Fig. 21. Number the strands mentally from 1 up to 32.

Now eight rows of square knots are to be tied all the way around the ring. Draw the knots in the first row up tight. Start the first row with strands 1, 2, 3, and 4; start the second row with strands 3, 4, 5, and 6; start the third row with strands 1, 2, 3, and 4, and so on.

Space the second row of knots about one-sixteenth of an inch from the first row. Space the third row about one-eighth of an inch from the second row. Space the fourth row about one-fourth of an inch from the third row. Space the fifth row about three-eighths of an inch from the fourth row. Then space each succeeding row about three-eighths of an inch from the row preceding it (Fig. 22).

When the eighth row of knots has been completed, make a flat of seven complete square knots with each group of four strands (Fig. 23).

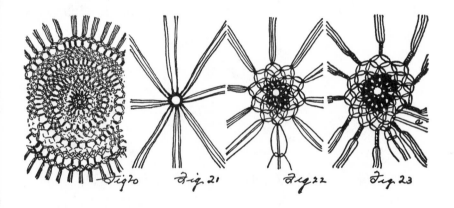

Fig. 20   Fig. 21   Fig. 22   Fig. 23

After making flats all the way around the piece, insert two double strands between each flat (Fig. 23, a). These are looped over the cords of the work already completed. With these strands make additional flats to match those already made. Then make more open mesh work, alternating with rows of flats, until the centerpiece is the desired width.

After making the last row of flats, tie one row of square knots around the centerpiece. Space this row of knots about three-eighths of an inch from the flats. This last row of square knots is tied with eight strands instead of four. This is done by using four central strands and tying the knots with the two strands on either side of the central strands.

The centerpiece is finished off with a fringe formed by cutting off all the strands to an equal length.

A SQUARE-KNOT HANDBAG

ONE of the most attractive types of square-knot handbags is
shown in Fig. 24.   It is made with two celluloid handbag rings,
which can be obtained at any department store, to serve as handles.
The knotting can be done with No. 1 D.M.C. Cordonnet, of which
four balls will be needed, or with two spools of silk thread known
as Silk Deluxe.   The illustration shows a bag made with 28 double
strands on each ring, but more can be used, and a bag of this type
made with 40 double strands on each ring is preferred by some
square-knot workers.

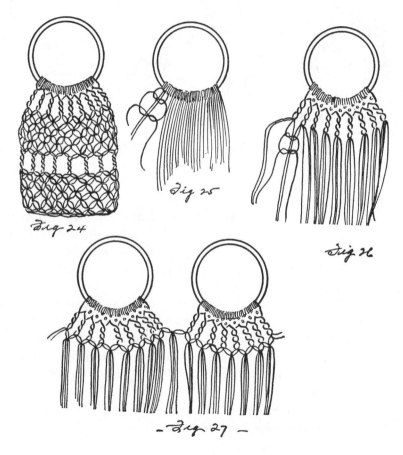

Fig. 24

Fig. 25

Fig. 26

Fig. 27

To make a bag with 28 double strands on each ring, cut 56 strands, each 50 inches long. Double each strand and loop 28 on each ring (Fig. 25). Pair off the strands on each ring in groups of four.

Start at the left and make two rows of square knots straight across. Use strands 1, 2, 3 and 4 in the first row, and strands 3, 4, 5, and 6 in the second row.

Continue by making a series of spirals about one and one-half inches long. (Fig. 26.)

Strands attached to each handle must now be joined or worked together (Fig. 27). This is done by taking the last two strands on each side of each handle and forming a square knot, with two central strands, and two outer strands (Fig. 27).

Next comes open mesh work. Space about three-eighths of an inch and make a row of square knots completely around the bag. Continue until there are six rows of open mesh work, spaced three-eighths of an inch apart. Then space three-eighths of an inch and make a row of spirals about one inch long. Once more, space three-eighths of an inch and make eight more rows of open mesh work, each row three-eighths of an inch from the preceding one.

Finish off the work at the bottom by making three more rows of square knots. Space the first row about one-fourth of an inch from the preceding row, the second row about one-eighth, and the third row about one-sixteenth of an inch.

The two sides of the bottom of the bag must now be joined together. Turn the bag inside out. Starting at the left, pick out the equal numbered strands on each side of the bag—strands 2, 4, 6, and so on. Make a row of square knots across the bottom of the bag, using the equal numbered strands as central strands, and the strands on either side for tying the knots. This joins both sides of the bag.

Complete the bag by extending the left-hand outside strand across the bottom and making two half hitches around it with each of the other strands. Extend the right-hand outside strand across the bottom of the bag and make two half hitches around it with each of the other strands. Then cut off the ends of the strands and the handbag will be completed.

NETTING AND SIMPLE KNOT-WORK

A NETTED CORD HAMMOCK

NETTING, or "natting," as it is sometimes called, is a fascinating occupation and, while a description of just how to do it is of necessity somewhat detailed, the actual process is simplicity itself and the work goes very quickly.

The principal equipment needed consists of a netting needle, or shuttle, which can be made at home or obtained at a department store, and a mesh stick. Figure 1 shows the shape and dimensions of the needle. If you wish to make your own, draw the outlines of the various parts on a piece of smooth, straight-grained ¼-inch pine, and cut out the body of the needle and the openings at each end with a coping saw, finishing with a knife, file, and sandpaper. To cut out the enclosed space near the pointed end, bore a ¼-inch hole near the right end of the opening, to provide a starting-place for the coping saw.

The mesh stick is shown in Fig. 2. These sticks can be obtained at many of the department stores; but are much easier to make than the needle, and can be shaped up at home from a piece of ¼-inch maple or other hard wood. If made at home, the edges should be carefully rounded and sandpapered very smooth.

For making the long meshes at both ends of the hammock, a measuring-board of the kind shown in Fig. 3 is needed. This is a board about 3 feet long, 4 inches wide, and 1 inch thick. A nail is driven into the board 2 inches from the left end, and about 1 inch from the far edge, as shown at A in the drawing. The location of the other nail, B, will be given later.

Seine twine, of 24-ply, is the best material of which to make the hammock, and you will need 1½ pounds. This twine comes in ½-pound skeins and should be wound into balls to keep it from knotting. This will make a hammock 12 feet long, with 8 feet of network in the center and 2 feet of cording at each end. In addition to the twine, you will need two galvanized iron rings, 2½ or 3 inches in diameter.

The first thing to do, once your equipment is ready, is to wind a long piece of cord on the needle. Start by looping the end of the cord around the tongue of the needle, as in Fig. 4. Then bring the cord down to the forked end of the needle and up the opposite side to the opening. Loop the cord around the tongue and bring it back on the same side as it was just brought up on to the forked end, then up and around the loop, and so on. Continue threading the needle in this way until it is full, which will be when it holds about 30 complete rounds.

To start making the long meshes at one end of the hammock, fasten one of the iron rings to the nail in the measuring-board by means of a short loop of string, as shown in Fig. 3. At a point 2 feet from the right-hand edge of the ring, drive a nail, B. Tie the end of the cord wound around the needle to the ring; bring the needle to the right and around the nail B; then bring it back and pass it through the ring from the under side. The cord will then be arranged as in Fig. 3.

Draw the cord up tightly. The next step is shown in Fig. 5. Put the left thumb on top of the cord where it crosses the ring, and hold the cord down tightly. Throw a loop of the cord over the thumb to the left and up over the center of the ring. Then pass the needle under the two long cords (between the ring and nail B), and bring it up over the left-hand cord of the loop, as in Fig. 5. Draw the looped knot thus formed tight under the thumb. Slip the strings off the nail B and tie them in an overhand knot 8 inches from the ring. This knot is tied chiefly to keep the two cords together and somewhat separate from the other meshes or loops that are to be ranged along-side them.

By the work just described, you have completed the first of the long meshes at one end of the hammock. Cut the cord, leaving a 6-inch long end, which later will be bound down alongside the meshes. Then make another long mesh or loop exactly as before. Continue until you have made 30 long meshes.

Now hang the ring by its short cord to a hook or nail driven into the wall. The hook should be a little above the level at which the knots of the netting are to be tied, so the distance of the hook from the floor will depend upon whether you are going to work standing up or sitting down.

Tie the end of the cord wound around the needle to the left out-

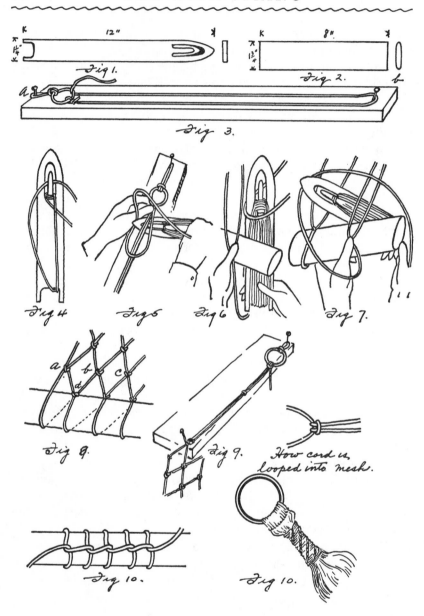

Fig 1.

Fig 2.

Fig 3.

Fig 4.   Fig 5.   Fig 6.   Fig 7.

Fig 8.

Fig 9.

How cord is looped into mesh.

Fig 10.

Fig 10.

side long loop or mesh (Fig. 6). While doing the netting, always work from left to right, and the first time across take care to keep the long meshes in their proper order; that is, in the order in which they are attached to the ring.

Now take the mesh stick in your left hand and place it at the lower end of the left outside long mesh, Fig. 6. Pass the cord (which was tied to the mesh) down over the mesh stick, and at the same time draw the lower end of the long mesh down until it rests on the upper side of the mesh stick. Put your left thumb against it to keep it from slipping (Fig. 6).

Pass the needle up through the next loop to the right and draw that loop down to the mesh stick. Move the thumb to the right and put it on the lower end of the second loop (Fig. 7). Throw the cord to the left over the thumb and across the second loop, as shown in Fig. 7, and pass the needle under both the cords of the second loop and up in front of the left-hand loop. Press your thumb down hard and draw the knot just formed up tight. This completes the first netting knot.

Continue by bringing the cord down across the front of the mesh stick, pass it up through the next mesh to the right, throw the loop over the thumb to the left, as in Fig. 7, pass the needle under the right-hand mesh, and draw the cord and knot tight as before. Work right across until all of the long meshes have been used and you have reached the right side. Turn the whole fabric over, and the cord attached to the needle will be on the left side ready to begin the second row of meshes. Slip the meshes already made off the mesh stick. (It is not necessary to keep the meshes on the mesh stick until an entire row is completed; they can be slipped off whenever the stick gets full.) When turning the fabric over, turn it over to the right and to the left alternately. This prevents twisting, which would take place if it were turned the same way each time.

The first mesh of each row is made a little differently from all the others. Fig. 8 will help to make the process clear. The knots A, B, and C are those just completed in the previous row. The cord is brought down over the front of the mesh stick and up through the first mesh, and the knot is tied as before (Fig. 7). When the loop is drawn tight, it may not draw to the mesh stick at its center, and a sidewise pull is necessary. This pull is made so the knots A and B are brought side by side. Then the knot at D may be tied. When the second mesh of the previous row is drawn down, it should pull directly into place, as should all the others that follow.

Continue netting until you have a net measuring 8 feet long for the central part of the hammock. When one winding of cord is used up, rewind the needle and fasten the new cord to the old with a square knot.

The next and final step is to make the long loops at the opposite end of the hammock and to fasten them to the second galvanized ring. The measuring board is used for this, but only to ensure all the loops being the same length. Make each loop from a separate piece of cord. Double each cord and loop the doubled part through a mesh as shown in Fig. 9. Then tie the two opposite ends together through the ring, using a square knot. Leave a 6-inch end, which can be bound down against the cords. Before tying the ends, tie an overhand knot in the center of the loop or mesh, as before. After the cords are looped through the mesh, put them over the nail B, Fig. 9. Then you will get each loop the correct length, which is 2 feet.

Use a piece of seine twine about 6 feet long to bind the ends of the long loops at each end of the hammock. Start close to the rings and bind the ends of the knots tightly down against the other cords. To prevent slipping, it is best to loop the cord under itself each time around, as shown in Fig. 10. The sides of the hammock may be strengthened by running a piece of rope through the outside row of meshes, and a knotted or netted fringe may also be added. Also, if you wish, you can put a wooden stretcher across each end of the netted part.

A TENNIS NET

FOR a tennis net you will need two pieces of manila or cotton rope, each 3/16 of an inch thick and 34 feet long. These are for the top and bottom of the net. For the meshes use hammock twine, of which you will need one and a half pounds. Two stakes, each five feet long, are needed for the ends of the net; two lengths of cotton rope for the guy-ropes, and four wooden pegs, each one foot long, for the guy-ropes. You will also need four wooden runners (Fig. 1), each 5 inches long, 1¼ inches wide, and about ½ inch thick, with holes bored near each end large enough to accommodate a guy rope.

For the netting, you will need a needle and mesh stick. The latter should be about 10 inches long, with a circumference of 3 inches. Take one of the 34-foot-long pieces of rope and tie a loop about 1-foot long in one end. Then place the loop over a hook or rod as shown in Fig. 2. Tie the end of the twine threaded on your needle to the bot-

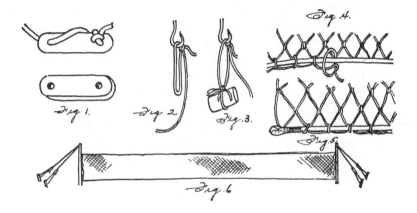

tom of the loop, as shown in Fig. 3; place the mesh stick behind the cord close up against the loop, and make the first mesh, by tying a weaver's knot in the manner already described. Continue netting until you have about 265 meshes, which makes a net of the correct width, 33 feet. As the work progresses and meshes accumulate on the stick, push them off to the left, a few at a time.

Begin the second row by placing the mesh stick under the first loop of the first row. Continue netting across the row, after each knot placing the mesh stick under the next loop to the right.

When it is necessary to rethread the needle, tie the ends of the old and new cords together with a square knot. Bind each end of the cord from the knot to the main cord with strong thread to make the join smooth and neat.

Continue netting until the net is 3 feet wide. Then untie the rope and spread out the net by sliding the knots apart. Fasten the second

34-foot-long rope to the bottom of the net as follows: Tie the rope to the first mesh with the cord threaded on the needle. Then carry the rope and cord to the next mesh, hold the rope, cord, and mesh firmly in place and throw the cord over your hand, passing the needle down through the mesh, under the rope, and out through the loop. This operation is shown in Fig. 4. Pull the cord tight and continue in the same manner across the net. Turn back the ends of the rope and bind them down with string (Fig. 5). In the same way, secure the ends of the rope at the top of the net.

To erect the net, set the two poles firmly in the ground a little over 33 feet apart; tie the net to the poles with eight pieces of twine, four at each end (Fig. 6); then drive the pegs into the ground, two pegs to each pole, about five feet from the pole (Fig. 6). Slide a runner on each end of the two guy-ropes by threading the rope through one of the holes in the runner, then passing the rope over the side down through the other hole, and fastening it with a knot (Fig. 1). Tie the guy-ropes around the tops of the poles, notching the poles to hold the ropes in place. Slip the loops made by the runners over the pegs, and tighten the ropes by pulling up the runners.

KNOTTED BAGS

BEAUTIFUL little shopping-bags, which make splendid presents, can be made from brightly colored pieces of string knotted together to form meshes.

The first step in making a bag such as the one shown in Fig. 1 is to make a string chain to serve as the edge or rim of the bag, such as is shown at A in the drawing. This can be made by one of the methods described in the section on "String Watch Chains." The two handles, by which the bag can be carried in the hand or over the arm, are made in the same manner and are sewed to the rim of the bag.

Another type of bag, such as that shown in Fig. 2, has a drawstring instead of handles. The drawstring is made by one of the methods used for making a string chain, as is the single handle.

For the bag shown in Fig. 1, make a chain 24 inches long for the rim, and sew its ends firmly together so it forms a circle. To facilitate making the knots in the body of the bag, this circle should be supported either on two nails driven into the wall or into a board, or on a piece of stiff cardboard cut to fit tightly inside the circle (Fig. 2a). The cardboard should be long enough to stretch the circle out to its full length. These supports are not absolutely necessary, but some people find it easier to do the knotting when the piece to which the knotted strings are attached is firmly held in place. Another and simpler way to accomplish this is to slip the circular chain over a bed post.

It will be necessary to have 24 pieces of light-weight cord or ordinary wrapping-string to make a bag with a circumference of 24 inches at the top. Each of these cords should be about 24 inches long. The center part of each string is knotted to the rim of the bag, so that two 12-inch strands hang down from the rim. The strings should be one inch apart.

Colored strings should be used and the most pleasing effect is obtained when the bag is made of two different colors. This is done by placing two strings of different colors side by side and knotting them to the rim as if they were a single string. Thus, four strings, instead of two, hang down from each knotted point on the rim, as indicated in Fig. 3.

If two colors are used, the string chains forming the rim or drawstring, and the handles, should be of the same two colors chosen for the body of the bag.

To facilitate the knotting and to ensure the meshes all being of the same size, a mesh stick should be used. This is a flat, thin piece of wood; an ordinary ruler will serve the purpose admirably. The stick should be about 12 or 15 inches long and 1¼ inches wide (Fig. 4) for a bag of the size described. Since the first or topmost row of knotting forms triangles only one-half as deep as the diamonds which are formed by the second and succeeding rows of knotting, it will also be necessary to have another mesh stick ⅝ of an inch wide, or just one-half as wide as the 1¼-inch stick to be used for making the body of the bag.

When ready to start knotting, place the ⅝-inch wide mesh stick between two of the sets of strings knotted to the rim piece (Fig. 5). Bring two of the strings together at the edge of the mesh stick near-

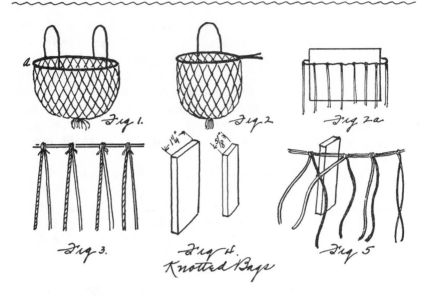

Fig. 1. Fig. 2 Fig. 2a

Fig. 3. Fig. 4. Knotted Bags Fig. 5

est to you and tie them together with a square or reef knot. If the bag is of two colors, as in Fig. 3, two strings from each knot are brought together and tied. The mesh stick is held between the knees while the knot is being tied, or, if someone is helping you, the mesh stick can be held by the other person.

When the first knot has been tied, remove the mesh stick and place it between the next strings to be knotted. Continue knotting in the same way until you have gone completely around the circle of the rim piece. This will complete the first or topmost row of the knotting. The second and succeeding rows, are made in exactly the same way, but the 1¼-inch mesh stick is used instead of the ⅝-inch stick.

Do not knot the cords all the way to the bottom; but leave about 2 inches unknotted at the end of each cord. Then, to complete the bag, knot the cords from the opposite sides together. Bind the free ends of the cords together, just beneath the bottom of the bag, and they will form a decorative tassel.

A PORTIÈRE

THIS portière can be made of light cord to be used in furnishing a doll's house or can be made of very heavy cord for use in a full-sized house or country cottage.

In the illustration the portière is made of twelve pieces of cord. Each piece is placed over the rod that is to support the finished portière so that one end hangs down on either side of the rod. The two parts of each cord are then tied together with a square knot a short distance below the rod, so a circular loop is formed around the rod.

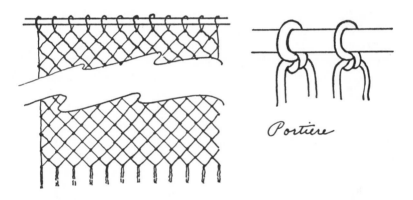

Portière

Square knots are used for fastening the cords together in their diamond pattern, and the drawing shows clearly how the knotting is done. The first time across, knot the far part of the left-hand cord to the near part of the cord next to it. Then knot the far part of this cord to the near part of the next cord, and so on. The second time across, the near part of the left-hand cord is knotted to the far part of the same cord. Then the near part of the second cord is knotted to its own far part, and so on.

When the portière is long enough, cut the ends to an even length. These ends may be frayed out to form tassels, or two or three overhand knots can be made in each cord.

A TIED OR KNOTTED CORD HAMMOCK

THE best knot to use for making a knotted string or twine hammock is the square or reef knot, which is easy to tie and absolutely will not slip, once it has been pulled tight. The kind of string used is important, since it must be sufficiently strong to bear the weight of the person lying in the hammock without giving way and letting him (or even worse, *her*) fall to the ground. About the best material for the purpose is 24-ply seine twine of medium-hard twist, and this can usually be obtained at stores that carry sporting-goods or fishing-equipment.

Each cord should be 18 feet long, and you will need 24 pairs of cords, or 48 cords all told. This measures out to 864 feet.

In addition to the cord you will need a rod or pole, which may be a broom handle or merely a straight piece of lumber, rounded or square, about 4 or 5 feet long. You will also need a mesh stick of the kind illustrated in Fig. 1. This is not difficult to make from two pieces of wood, and will make the work of knot-tying very much easier than if no such device were utilized. The upright board should be of convenient height for a person sitting in a chair. One foot is rested on the baseboard to hold the stick steady while the knots are being tied. For tying the first row of knots on each side of the center stick, you will need a mesh stick which is only 1⅞ inches from front to back, instead of 3½ inches, like the big mesh stick. A small stick that can be held between the knees or by some other person can be used for this purpose (Fig. 1).

When all the cords are ready, arrange them in pairs—24 pairs all told—and loop the center of each pair around the broomstick, as shown in Figs. 2 and 3. This is done because it would be difficult, when knotting, to pull the full length of each cord through each knot. With the cords fastened to the stick at their centers, you knot one half of the hammock at a time, knotting from the center toward each end, one half being knotted, and then the other. Even half the length of each cord is too long to draw through each knot without inconvenience, so, as shown in Fig. 3, it is well to wind each pair of cords around the fingers into a little bundle which is secured with a half hitch and left hanging from the stick. The cords on the side of the hammock which is not being knotted should be looped over a hook or nail, as shown in Fig. 3, or be kept out of the way in some other manner.

One more thing remains to be done before commencing to tie the knots. This is to fasten the center broom-handle stick in some way, so it will not have to be supported by the hands. If you have a low work bench or a box of the proper size (about 3½ or 4 feet high), the stick can be laid upon it and held in place with nails driven on either side of it. Another method is to fasten it to nails driven into the wall by means of two pieces of rope, one tied to each end of the stick. Failing either of these methods, the stick can be laid on the floor and secured with nails driven into the floor on either side of it. In this case, you will work sitting on the floor, and the upright of the mesh stick need be only about 12 inches high.

Once the center stick has been secured in place, so it will not move about when you pull against it while tying the knots, you are ready to begin. The first time across, the two cords forming each pair are tied together, as A and B and C and D in Fig. 2. Place the small mesh stick between cords A and B and tie them together, close up against the stick, with a square knot, as shown in Fig. 4. Pull the knot up tight so it will be certain not to loosen and slip. Remove the mesh stick, place it between cords C and D, and tie them together in the same way, and continue across until each of the 24 pairs have been knotted together.

When starting the second row, place the large mesh stick between cords B and C, and tie these two cords together (Fig. 5). Then place the stick between cords D and E and tie them together, continuing in this manner all the way across. This process knots the pairs of cords together instead of knotting the two cords of the same pair.

The third time across the combinations are the same as in the first row; that is, the two cords of each pair of cords, as A and B, and C and D, are tied together. The large mesh stick is used on all but the first row and ensures the meshes all being the same size. The alternation of rows is continued until the cords are knotted to within 2½ feet of their ends.

When this stage has been reached, pull out the center stick and

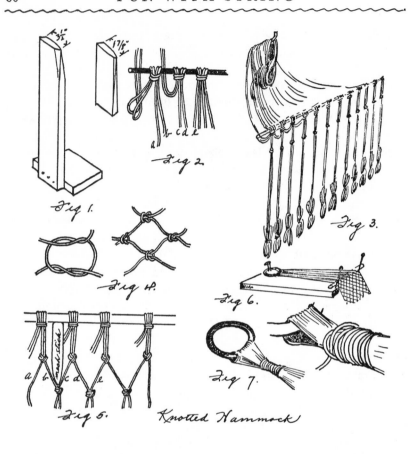

insert it in the second row of meshes. Take down the cords that were looped over the hook, and begin the knotting of the second half of the hammock. Use the small mesh stick to complete the first, or center, line of meshes. Then continue with the large mesh stick. Knot the cords to within 2½ feet of their ends, as before. Then remove the center stick and insert it in the last, or end row, of the meshes.

The cords at each end of the hammock are now to be made fast to a galvanized iron ring about 2½ or 3 inches in diameter. These can be obtained at any hardware store. Drive a nail in the floor, if this is practicable, or else into a board on the top of a box, and put one of the rings over the nail. At a distance of 2 feet from the ring, drive two nails to hold the stick in position while the cords are being tied to the ring. These nails keep the stick and ring equidistant during the tying and ensure all the lengths of cord between the stick and ring being the same length (Fig. 6).

Bring each pair of cords to the ring. Pass one cord under and one over the ring and tie them together with a square knot. Repeat with each pair of cords until all are tied. Bring the short ends of the cords, which are left after the tying has been completed, back to the main body of the cord and bind them with an extra piece of cord or string. Start the binding by looping the end of the extra cord tightly with a square knot. Then wind the extra cord tightly around the other cords for a distance of about 2 inches. Each time the cord is wound around, pass the end through its own loop or winding and draw it tight (Fig. 7). Finish the binding by giving the cord a double looping through its own winding. Then insert an awl or other sharp-pointed tool underneath the wound cord, push the free end of the cord back through the small opening made by the awl, and bring the end up and out between the cord at the center of the binding. This will keep the binding from coming undone when the hammock is in use.

The sides of the hammock can be finished off by binding them with wide tape, or a rope can be passed lengthwise through the two outside rows of meshes. If desired, a fringe can be added to each side, made by knotting cords into a mesh in exactly the same manner as that employed for making the body of the hammock.

A FISH NET

A HANDLE for a fish net can be purchased at a sporting-goods store or can be home-made. If you make your own handle, you can form the circular part from a piece of stiff wire, and bind this part to a wooden handle with copper wire. A handle entirely of wood can be made by cutting down a small sapling having branches forming a Y (Fig. 1). Flatten the ends of the Y on one side with your knife. Then soak the forks of the Y in water for half a day so they will bend easily without breaking. Bend the two flattened ends until they lap each other and lash or bind the parts together at five different points, as shown in Fig. 1.

Fish line, seine cord or any strong smooth-finished twine can be used for the net. Cut a number of pieces, each a little longer than twice the depth of the net. A good average depth is 20 inches. For such a net cut the cords about 45 inches long.

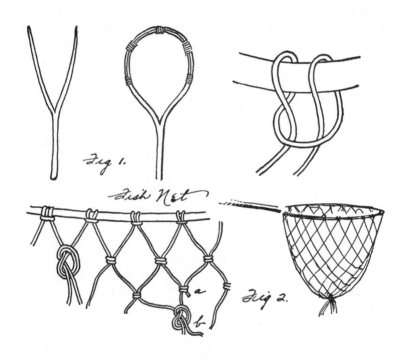

Fig. 1.

Fish Net

Fig. 2.

Loop the cords on the round part of the handle as shown in Fig. 2. Then knot the cords all the way around as explained in the description of how to make a knotted hammock. You may use mesh sticks or not, just as you prefer. Many people find it easy to make the meshes all the same size without using a stick for measuring. If you do use mesh sticks, you will need two—one with a width equal to that of the depth of the diamond-shaped meshes which form the body of the net, and one just one-half as wide to use when making the first row of meshes which are half-diamonds.

To draw the net in toward the bottom, you must cut off some of the strings in each row, as shown at A and B, Fig. 2, making the knot as shown at B.   In this way the number of meshes is gradually reduced until they all meet and close the bottom.

USEFUL THINGS MADE WITH
ROPE AND STRING

CLOTHES-ROPE RUGS

VERY good-looking and serviceable rugs of the same types as those made of braided jute yarn can be made from ordinary clothes rope or sash cord. These are not so much work, of course, as the braided rugs, since there is no plaiting to be done.

Prepare the clothes-line by soaking it in water to remove the kinks and to make it pliable. Then, if you wish a colored rug, you must dye the rope, using regular dress dyes for this purpose. The rug may be all one color or, by dyeing pieces of different lengths different colors, you can make a rug with rows or coils of contrasting colors. Apart from the dyeing, the only work that requires real care in making such a rug is the sewing of the coils or strips together. Carpet thread should be used for this, and care should be taken that the sewing is done evenly so the rug will lie flat when it is completed. You will need a strong needle—a sail-maker's needle is best—for needle and thread must be pushed through the center of the rope. It will help in the sewing if you use a small block of wood to press against the end of the needle when it is passing through the rope. A sailor's "palm" is ideal for this kind of work and should be used if you can obtain one. They are sold by ship chandlers.

Instead of sewing a rectangular rug of this kind by passing the carpet thread through the centers of the various pieces of rope, the pieces can be bound together by means of string. Such a rug is shown in Fig. 1, in which dark-colored strings have been used to provide a contrast with the body of the rug, which is made with pieces of undyed clothes rope. The string is passed around the ropes, as shown at A. The strings must be pulled good and tight in order to give the rug a firm surface; but care must be taken not to pull them so tight as to cause the ropes to ride up on each other. If the rug requires a greater amount of rigidity than is supplied by the strings, it can be sewed to a base-piece of canvas or burlap.

Fig. 2 shows several designs for rugs in which the rope is sewed in place. The effect of these designs is greatly increased if two or more colors are used. The oval rug is probably the simplest to make, as there are no definite corners to shape. The three S-shaped scrolls at the center are made from three separate pieces of rope. Each scroll has two coils, each of which should measure about 3 inches across. Mark the center of each piece of rope by tying a piece of twine around it to indicate the end of the first coil and the beginning of the second. Coil one of the ends around tightly three times and then commence to stitch the rows together. Pass the needle from the outer edge to the center of the coil, leaving the end of the thread protruding. From the center, go to the outer edge again about 1 inch away from the starting-point. Tie the thread to the protruding end to secure it.

Continue in the same way, keeping the stitches about 1 inch apart along the outer edge, until the starting-point is reached. Then continue the coiling, and secure the rows in the same way, sewing each row to the previous row, as far as the piece of twine which marks the center of the rope. With the remaining half of the rope, make another coil so that the two, when finished, are in the form of a letter S.

When the three scrolls are completed, it is best to nail them temporarily to a board to keep them in position while the surrounding rows are added. To make sure that the scrolls are in a perfectly straight line, a pencil line can be drawn on the board as a guide.

Commence winding the border of the rug at one end of the row of scrolls, A, Fig. 2, and sew the rope to the scrolls, passing the needle through two rolls of the scrolls to make the fastening quite secure. As the winding continues, sew each row to the preceding row. When about four rows have been completed and the shape of the rug is well defined, it can be taken off the board; but the work should be continued on a flat surface to ensure the finished rug being flat. Continue adding rows until the rug is the size you wish it to be.

The center of the round rug is an easy-to-make coil. Coil the rope three times and then start sewing the coils together, taking care to get a good circular shape. The S-shaped scrolls are made in the same way as those described in connection with the oval rug, and are sewed to the center coil. It is much easier to do this if the coil is first nailed to a board and kept there until the scrolls and a few additional outer coils of rope have been added. This helps a great deal to ensure the rug having the right shape. When it has been removed from the board, continue adding the rows of rope, working on a flat surface such as a table or the floor, until the rug has reached the required size.

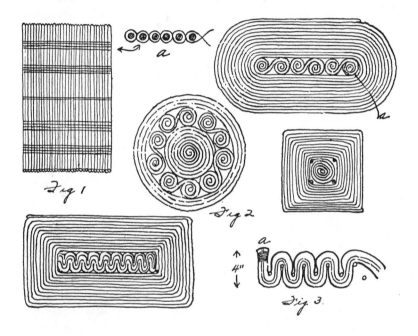

Fig 1

Fig 2

Fig 3.

The square rug is started with a coil in exactly the same way as the circular rug. When the coil measures about 8 or 9 inches across, the square shape of the mat is started. The coil should be nailed to a board while the first few square border rows are being added. Then four nails are driven into the board, one at each corner of the inner, or first, row of the square part. The first row of rope is sewed securely to the coil at the center of each side. The second row is sewed to the first, but at the center of the sides the stitches should be carried through to the central coil to make it more secure. If you find it difficult to make the corners square, the rope can be cut part-way through at each corner.

The rectangular rug has a very attractive zigzag central design. This is made from three pieces of rope and is worked on a board, as shown in Fig. 3. Draw two pencil lines 4 inches apart (the width of the zigzag), and drive nails into the board at 1¼-inch intervals and ¾ of an inch in from the lines, to mark the turning-points of the zigzag. Bind the ends of three pieces of clothes rope together, nail them to the board at A, and pass the ropes around the nails as shown, until the required length of zigzag has been made. This will be about 18 inches. Bind the ends of the ropes and nail them to the board, and the zigzag will be ready for sewing together. Pass the needle through the ropes, just below the top row of nails, and then just above the bottom row. Then pass it through the center of the zigzag in between the two first rows.

The body of the rug is wound and sewed in the same way as described for the oval rug, the first row being sewed to the points of the zigzag. When a few rows have been completed, the rug can be taken from the board and continued on a flat surface.

SPOOL KNITTING

A NUMBER of useful things can be made with the help of a spool knitter, including good-looking handles or drawstrings for bags, skipping-ropes, reins for small children to play with, and belts knitted from lengths of heavy cord.

The first step is to make the knitting spool, and this will take only a few minutes. Get a large empty spool—the kind that is used to hold the strongest sewing-thread. Around the hole in one end of the spool, drive either three, four or five brads. The process of knitting is the same, whatever the number of brads; but five brads will produce a firmer, more solid rope than three. Drive the brads in straight, leaving about ⅜ of an inch of their length projecting.

Any kind of string may be used for spool knitting. Thin string will produce a thin knitted chain, naturally, while heavier string will make a thicker and stronger chain.

Start the knitting by putting the end of the string down through the hole in the spool. In the drawing, the brads are marked A, B, and C and D. Pass the string around A, then B, then C, and then D. Bring the string again around A, over the first loop, as shown. With a long sharp pin, lift the first or lower loop, E, over the second or upper loop. This brings loop E inside the brad and leaves the upper loop outside the brad. Keep the string which passes through the hole in the spool pulled taut.

Continue by passing the string around brad B, then lift the lower loop of string over brad B. Carry the string around to C and lift the lower loop over brad C. Continue in the same manner round and round the spool. The rope or chain which takes shape passes down through the hole in the spool. When the rope is as long as you want it to be, fasten the end of the string by threading it up through each outside loop in turn.

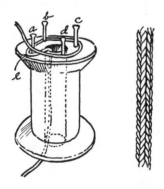

Some people prefer to use small staples instead of brads, and if you can get staples, you may find it easier to lift the strings over them.

An interesting-looking chain can be made by using white string for knitting and passing a colored string down through the hole in the spool. The colored string does not have to be touched. Simply knit as described above and when the chain is finished, the colored string will be inside and will show through. Your friends will be very puzzled, and will wonder how you made this chain.

WATCH-CHAINS MADE OF STRING

EVERY so often, with a greater or lesser degree of regularity, the fad for making watch-fobs of string or shoe-strings becomes popular, and boys and girls everywhere make them of every conceivable combination of colors. They are really very decorative little gadgets, and are always suitable to use as birthday or Christmas presents. Directions for making several types of string chains, some of which may be new to readers, are given in this section. These chains may also be used for handles of knotted string bags, and as hat cords, whistle lanyards, dog leashes, children's reins, and belts.

The apparatus needed for making the watch-fob shown in Fig. 3 is a ½-inch square piece of cardboard with four holes punched in it, as shown in the drawings. The four pieces of cord, which may be all the same color, or of two or four contrasting colors, are tied together at one end and are then threaded through the holes, as shown in Fig. 1. The method of plaiting the cords is illustrated in Fig. 2. The strings simply cross each other at right angles, and you may begin with any one of them. The fourth and last cord is pushed under the looped end of the first cord; the others are bent or passed over the cord next to them.

When you have made the square shown in Fig. 2, keep right on making the same simple plait, continuing with the cord that you started with. When the chain has reached the desired length, finish it off by sewing the ends of the cords together with thread, or, if you prefer, bind the ends together with thread and fray the cords out to form a tassel. The chain may be attached to a watch by means of a piece of string passed under the knotted ends of the cord and tied to the handle of the watch, or a catch such as the one shown in Fig. 3 can be purchased at the ten-cent store and sewed securely to the knotted ends of the chain.

These watch-fobs can also be made with shoe-strings, in which event they have a square shape, rather than the cylindrical shape that results when string or cord is used.

The watch-fob shown in Fig. 5 is even more simple to make than the one just described. The thickness of the chain depends on the thickness of the string and the number of strings employed. Either

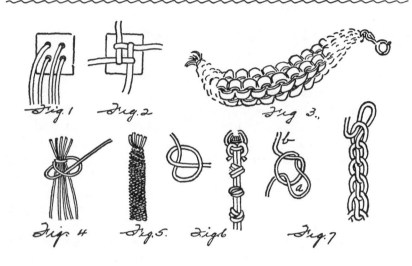

Fig. 1   Fig. 2   Fig. 3.

Fig. 4   Fig. 5.   Fig. 6   Fig. 7

six or eight are generally used, though ten or even twelve may be made use of. The string should be quite thick in order to make a substantial chain, and the appearance of the chain is heightened by the use of strings of contrasting colors. Each string should be about 1 foot long for a medium-sized chain four or five inches long.

Tie the ends of the strings together with a single knot. Then select one string—it makes no difference which one—and tie it around the other strings close to the knotted end. Take the free end of the string in your right hand, pass it around the other strings, and pass the end through the loop formed by the encircling string, as shown in Fig. 4. Draw the knot tight by pulling on the free end of the string. Repeat this operation until you come to the end of the first string; then continue with one of the other strings, keeping on until each of the strings has been used. In the completed chain, the knots will be found to follow one another in a spiral that runs the length of the chain.

An easily made two color chain is shown in Fig. 6. This is made of two pieces of thick cord of contrasting colors. Knot the cords together at one end, and then tie another knot about 1 inch from the end, so there will be a loop which can be passed through the watch handle, as shown in the drawing. The chain is then made by tying overhand knots in the cords at intervals of about ¼ of an inch. When the chain has been made the desired length, the ends of the cords can be frayed out to form a tassel.

Another interesting and good-looking chain is made by using the form of chain stitch illustrated in Fig. 7. A circle is made at one end of the cord in the same manner as the one for the overhand knot; but instead of passing the end of the cord through the circle, the cord is doubled into a loop and the loop is passed through. This loop is shown at A in the drawing. To continue with the chain, take the free part of the cord B, double it to form a loop and pass it through loop A. Draw on the second loop until loop A is snugged down tight; then continue with the chain by repeating this process. When the chain is long enough, it is made secure and kept from becoming undone by passing the end through the last loop and drawing it tight.

FLAT PLAITED CORD BELTS

Heavy, tightly twisted cord is used for making the flat plaited belt strands shown in Fig. 1. The strands illustrated are made, from left to right, of seven, seven, nine, and eleven cords. If differently colored cords are used, the resulting designs will be exceptionally good-looking. The belts can be fastened with an ordinary buckle and a cloth or leather tongue containing one or more holes, or by means of any of the other types of fasteners that are obtainable today in the department and five-and-ten cent stores. If a buckle is used, it will be possible to fasten one end of each cord to the cross-bar of the buckle. Tie the cords to the bar by means of square knots. If some other kind of fastener is used, it may be necessary to sew one part of it to a piece of heavy linen or other cloth and also sew one end of each cord to the same material so they will be held firmly in place during the plaiting. If you wish, you can use stout cords for fastening the belt, tying the cords together to keep the belt in place around your waist. If this is done, a piece of heavy cloth is sewed to each end of the plait, and the fastening cords are sewed to the same piece of material.

The two left-hand plaits shown in Fig. 1 are made with seven cords. The first is a simple over one and under one weave, and the way to make it is clearly shown in the illustration. The second plait is a herring-bone pattern which is woven by carrying the cords over two and under two.

Fig 1.   *Fig 2*

The third plait, made with nine cords, is woven by carrying each cord under two, over one, and then under one and over two. The fourth plait, made with eleven cords, is made by carrying each cord under two, over two, under two, and over two. By following the drawings and keeping carefully in mind the number of adjoining cords that must be passed over or under, you will have no difficulty in weaving any of these handsome plaits.

When a plait has been made the desired length, the ends of the cords are doubled back on the plait and sewed securely to the plait to prevent unraveling.

These plaits also make very good-looking hat-bands for hats of the Boy Scout type. When used for this purpose, the two ends of the plait are sewed to a piece of strong linen or other cloth and, when this has been done, the ends themselves are also sewed together to make certain of a good strong join.

HOW TO CUT A STRING WITHOUT KNIFE OR SCISSORS

THIS method of cutting, or breaking, a good strong piece of cord may frequently be a very useful accomplishment, when one's knife or scissors have been lost or mislaid. Even a really stout piece of string or cord can be broken by this method without hurting the hands.

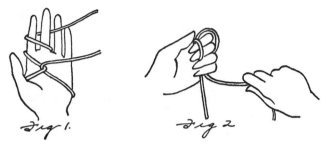

Take the cord and pass it around the left hand, as shown in Fig. 1, so as to form a cross or double loop over the palm. One end is then wound around the fingers, and the other taken in the right hand. Then, by closing both hands, and giving a very sharp, quick pull, the string will be broken at the cross in the left hand.

A ROPE TREE CLIMBER

BY THE use of this easily made rope-climbing apparatus, you can climb right up the trunk of a tree, without any branches to give you handholds. The climber is very similar to those used by the Pacific Island natives for climbing their tall, slender palm trees.

The climber can be made from ordinary clothes-line—Number 7 or stronger—or can be made from regular hemp rope ½ inch or more in diameter. The chief point is to use rope that is without question strong enough to bear your weight and to withstand chafing against the trunk of the tree. A piece of rope about 4 feet long is of a size that will fit almost any average-sized tree.

The climber is made anew for each tree that is to be climbed. The rope is passed around the tree and is then securely knotted some distance from its two ends with one or two square knots. The loop thus formed should have a somewhat larger circumference than that of the tree trunk. The two ends of the rope are now tied together to form a smaller loop just large enough to accommodate one of your feet. The knots used should be square knots, which absolutely will not slip once they are tightened.

To use the climber, after it has been fastened around the tree, raise it off the ground about two feet, place your right foot in the small loop, and grasp the tree as you would in ordinary climbing.

Now draw the foot up as far as you can and draw up the rope on the far side of the tree at the same time with one of your hands. The process of pulling up the rope can be simplified to a considerable extent by fastening a short length of rope to the far side of the loop surrounding the tree. The free end of this rope is held in one of the hands and each time the foot is moved upward, the loop is simultaneously pulled up by the rope "handle."

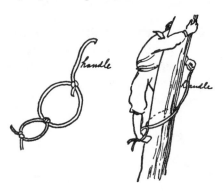

Once the loop has been pulled up, it will catch and bind against the tree trunk, permitting you to stand upright and at ease for as long as you wish. When you are ready for another upward step, draw your right foot and the rope upward, and repeat the process until you have reached the lower branches of the tree.

Climbing with this device is a real thrill and, provided that square knots are used and pulled tight when making the climber, there is absolutely no danger.

AN ANTI-SLAM DEVICE

THIS anti-slam device, which is easily made from a short piece of rope, will be welcomed in many households. The device will not only keep a door from being slammed, but will prevent it from being entirely closed.

The anti-slammer is made by forming loops on the ends of a short length of rope. The doubled-over ends are bound to the main body of the rope by means of cord or twine tightly wrapped around.

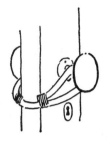

When the device is in use, the two loops are fitted over the door knobs on each side of the door, as shown in the drawing, and the central portion of the rope forms a cushion which prevents the door from slamming.

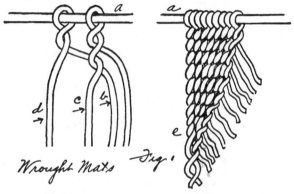

Wrought Mats — Fig. 1

WROUGHT MATS

WROUGHT mats for floor use are made with manila rope; smaller mats for table use may be made with seine cord. They are exceptionally attractive and, since the passing of the old-time sailing ships, the art of making them has become almost forgotten.

Fig. 1 shows very clearly the method employed. A piece of rope, a, is stretched tightly in a horizontal position, and other pieces of rope or cord of the size and length required for the finished mat are hung over it as shown, their centers resting on the horizontal rope.

Two people are required to make the mat, one standing on each side of the horizontal rope. The left-hand rope is twisted around itself as shown, and one part is given to the person opposite. The next rope is then twisted in the same manner and one end is given to the person opposite. The remaining end, b, is twisted around the left-hand rope, c, and c is then twisted around the other part of the left-hand rope, d.

The weaving or twisting is continued in the same manner until all the ropes have been worked in. The two ropes at the left, e, are always twisted together, until those to the right are worked into them. At the bottom, another piece of rope similar to the one used at the top is put in. The strands of the ropes forming the surface of the mat are then separated and are hitched around the bottom rope. The loose ends are worked under the twisted ropes by means of an awl or other sharp-pointed instrument.

To make the surface of these mats softer, sailors cut a number of strands of old manila rope, each about 3 inches in length, push these through the divisions of the twists, and then open out the strands.

INDIAN BELTS

THESE belts can be made in a wide range of colors and Indian designs, and are among the most attractive articles that can be made with cord work. The material recommended is No. 120 Dreadnaught Cord, which can be purchased by name at department stores. For each of the belts described, you will need two hanks of this cord, each of a different color. In addition, you will need a belt buckle with an inside width of $\frac{5}{8}$ of an inch. For the sake of convenience, it will be assumed that you are going to make a blue and white belt, and the description will refer to these two colors. Dreadnaught Cord, however, comes in all colors, and any combination of colors may be used.

Cut two lengths of white and two lengths of blue cord, each 8 feet long. This is a convenient length to start with and as the original cords are reduced to about 6-inch lengths, new cords are added as described later. The belts can also be made without adding new cords, in which case the original cords should be cut 24 feet long. This makes a belt 32 inches in length.

Double each cord and loop them over the center bar of the buckle, as shown in Fig. 1. The arrangement of the cords by colors differs according to the design. The different arrangements are given below. When the cords have been looped in place, turn the buckle over so the tongue points downward. This makes it easier to start knotting the belt. Then put the buckle over a hook driven into the wall, a nail driven into the floor, or arrange by some other means to hold it firmly in place.

The knot used in making the belt is a simple slip knot, of the type illustrated in Fig. 2. This knot is always made over one of the other cords, which we shall call the filler. After each knot is made, it should be drawn up tightly, but care should be taken not to let the filler buckle up. One other point—the knots are always made two at a time with the same cord over the filler, the second knot binding the first in place.

There are two methods of knotting the belt. We will call these Method 1 and Method 2.

Method 1

Take the left-hand cord in the right hand and cross it over the next three cords. Keep it parallel to the center bar of the buckle. Use this cord as a filler and, with the left hand, knot the next three cords over it, making two knots with each cord. Be sure to keep the filler taut so it will not buckle up. Next take the right-hand cord in the left hand and cross it over the three cords to its left, keeping it parallel to the center bar of the buckle. Use this cord as a filler and knot the three cords to its left over it, one after the other, making two knots with each cord.

The two fillers will now meet in the center. Cross them, keeping the right-hand one on top, and make two knots over it with the left-hand filler. This completes one full row knotted by Method 1.

Method 2

Cross the two middle cords, keeping the right-hand one on top, and make two knots over it with the left-hand cord. One of the mid-

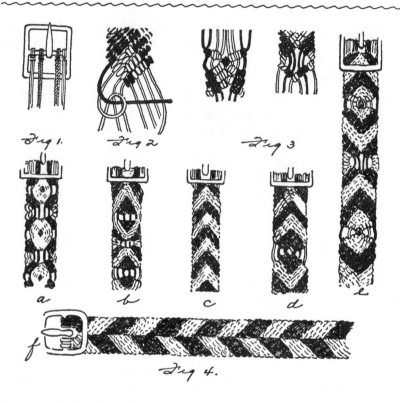

Fig 1.   Fig 2.   Fig 3.

a   b   c   d   e

f   Fig 4.

dle cords will now be found to be pointing to the left and one to the right. Take the one pointing to the left in the left hand and cross it over the three cords on the left side of the belt. Hold it so it points on a downward angle and use it as a filler, knotting the three cords over it, one after the other, and making two knots with each cord. Then take the cord pointing to the right, cross it over the three cords on the right of the belt and knot the cords over it in the same manner, keeping the filler pointed on a downward angle.

This completes one full row knotted by Method 2. Care must be taken in making the second and succeeding rows by this method first to cross and knot the two middle cords, as explained at the beginning.

CHANGING FROM ONE METHOD TO
THE OTHER

WHEN changing from Method 1 to Method 2, it is not necessary to cross and knot the two middle cords, as these cords will be found to be already properly crossed and knotted. In the succeeding rows knotted by Method 2, however, it is essential that the two middle cords be crossed and knotted.

Fig. 3 shows at the left the design that takes shape when Method 2 is joined to Method 1. The drawing at the right shows the design when Method 1 is joined to Method 2.

ADDING NEW CORDS

WHEN working with Method 1, cross the left-hand cord over the next three cords in the usual way and make two knots over it with the first cord. Before knotting the second cord place a new cord, about 6 feet long, beside the filler, with its end passing under the first cord and extending about 4 inches beyond the edge of the belt. This makes a double filler. Knot the second and third cords over both of them. Repeat the process, using the right-hand cord as filler.

The four fillers will now meet in the center. Pass the two short ones to the back and join the two new long ones in the usual manner, keeping the right-hand one on top and making two knots over it with the left-hand one. Do not pull too hard on the new fillers until they have been knotted together.

Now make another row in the regular way, and then turn the belt over and cut off the ends of the two cords close to the belt.

New cords are added on the same principle when working with Method 2.

ENDING THE BELT

A BELT can only be ended in a point when it is being knotted by Method 1. Take the two left-hand cords, use them together as a filler, and knot the next two cords over them in the usual way. Draw the knots up tightly. Do the same thing from the right side. Four fillers will now meet in the center. Drop two of them to the back and knot the other two in the usual way. Repeat this on the next row. All the cords will now be bunched together. Turn them all to the back and with a large needle and strong thread, sew them all to the back of the belt. Then cut off the ends of all the cords.

BELT DESIGNS

The following figures show six different belt designs, and the text describes the method of arranging the differently colored cords and the methods of knotting to produce each design.

Fig. A

Place one cord of white on each side of the buckle and the two cords of blue in the middle.

Make three rows with Method 1 and then three rows with Method 2. Repeat until the belt is made the desired length.

Fig. B

The cords are arranged in the same manner as in Fig. A. Make five rows with Method 1 and then five rows with Method 2. Repeat until the belt is the desired length.

Fig. C

The cords are arranged as in Fig. A. Make the entire belt with Method 1. In this design there will be no buckle holes, but the tongue of the buckle can easily be inserted through the belt between the knots.

Fig. D

The cords are arranged as in Fig. A. Make nine rows with Method 1 and then nine rows with Method 2. Repeat until the belt is the desired length.

Fig. E

The cords are arranged as in Fig. A. Make seven rows with Method 1 and then seven rows with Method 2. Repeat until the belt is the desired length.

Fig. F

Put the two white cords on one side of the buckle and the two blue cords on the other side. Make the entire belt with Method 1.

In the first five designs three colors, such as red, white and blue can be used by arranging the cords as follows: Put one red cord on each side of the buckle. Then take the blue cord and, in passing the loop over the center bar of the buckle, put it over the tongue of the buckle so it is exactly in the center. Pass the white cord over the tongue of the buckle also, but in drawing the ends of the cord through the loop allow the knot to spread so that it sets over the blue cords. The single strings should then be arranged as follows— red, white, blue; blue, white, red.

The belts can also be made wider by using a wider buckle and additional cords. The method of knotting remains the same.

HOW TO MAKE AND THROW A LARIAT

A LARIAT for throwing should never be made from clothes-line, as many boys have found out to their sorrow. Good manila rope should be used, and it should be $\frac{3}{8}$-inch thick and 35 feet long. For rope spinning, lariats are made of braided cotton sash cord; but these lariats are never used for throwing or lassoing.

The method of forming the eye, or honda, at the end of the rope is shown in Figs. 1 and 2. Tie an overhand knot as in Fig. 1, and pass the end through as shown in Fig. 2. Then tie an overhand knot on the end of the rope to keep it from pulling out. The two knots should be jammed together as tightly as possible, and the eye should be from 3 to 4 inches long. Pass the opposite end of the rope through the eye, and the lariat will be completed and ready for use.

Wire can be wound around the eye at the end if desired. It prevents wear and adds a little weight, which helps somewhat when throwing the lariat.

The eye can also be formed by making an eye splice. This is just as good a method as the one described above and the fact that it is not commonly used by cowboys is because they do not know how to make the splice.

THROWING THE LARIAT

THE first step in throwing a lariat is to shake out a noose about 4 or 5 feet long, as in Fig. 3. The eye of the lariat should be a little more than half way down the side of the noose and must be on the outer side of the noose, as shown.

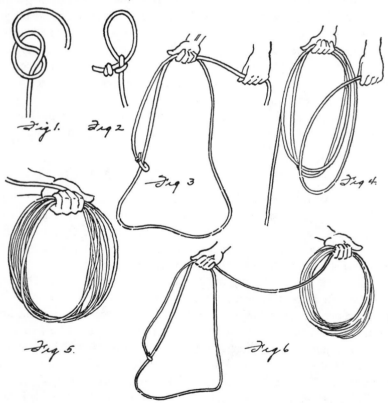

Fig. 1.   Fig. 2   Fig. 3   Fig. 4.   Fig. 5.   Fig. 6

The next step is to coil up the lariat. This is done with the left hand, the coils being taken in the right hand (Fig. 4). Each coil should be about 15 inches long. When the coiling is completed, the coils are transferred to the left hand. The end of the rope is held between the left thumb and forefinger, as shown in Fig. 5.

You are now ready for the throw and should stand as shown in Fig. 6. Swing the noose up and around overhead, swinging it from right to left. As you swing the noose, you can let out more rope until the weight feels right for throwing.

When beginning, stand about 10 feet from the object you are going to try to lasso. A post is one of the best objects upon which to practice. Keep your eye glued right to the top of the post and throw the noose straight at that point. When you are ready to throw, step straight toward the post and throw. Practice at a distance of 10 feet until you can lasso the post every time, or nearly every time; then gradually work back to 30 feet. This is the usual maximum distance for roping, although some expert cowboys can sometimes rope calves at forty or even fifty feet.

If you find that the noose does not open out when you are swinging it around your head, this will probably be due to the fact that the rope is twisted. To get the twists out, slide the eye down to the end, take it in your hand, unwind the rope and shake out the twists. This is the only way to straighten out the rope.

WEAVING

WEAVING with colored twine or jute yarn is good fun, and you can make any number of interesting and decorative things. Small mats can be made for use on tables and bureaus; rugs can be made for a doll's house; good-looking handbags are not difficult to weave and very nice to have, and, in short, people who like this kind of work, or play, can enjoy themselves for hours with simple cardboard looms and a few balls of twine. For weaving you can use soft finish cotton string, jute yarn, or firmer kinds of string such as seine cord. Each kind of string gives a different texture and a larger or smaller weave, according to its size.

A CARDBOARD LOOM FOR WEAVING SQUARE
AND OBLONG FABRICS

FIG. 1 shows a simple type of cardboard loom on which can be woven string mats, handbags, and other articles that are square or oblong in shape. The loom can be made from the cover of a cardboard box, the cardboard piece on the back of a pad, or from any other piece of stout cardboard that will not easily bend or break. A

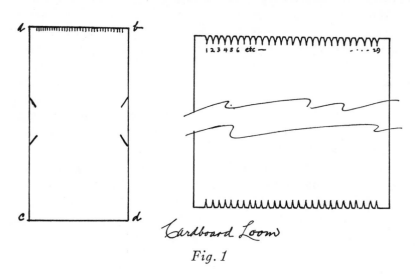

Fig. 1

good average size suitable for the weaving of small and medium-sized articles would be a piece of cardboard measuring about 15 inches long and 8 to 10 inches wide.

At each end, ¼-inch in from the end, measure in ½ inch from the left side and mark with a pencil dot. Then mark every ¼ inch across the loom, stopping ½ inch from the right side. Then notch the ends as shown. It is a good idea to number the notches at both ends, as this will help you when you thread the loom. Make two ½-inch slanting cuts on each side, which are to hold the ends of the warp strings, and the loom is completed and ready for use.

A HAND-WOVEN BAG

To MAKE a bag like the one shown in Fig. 1, the loom should be threaded with 21 warp strings. Used tightly twisted cord for the warp strings, as these will make the sides of the bag firm and able to hold their shape well. Jute yarn is recommended for the weft, although heavy string or cord can also be used with very good results. The bag shown in Fig. 1 is made, for the most part, of light or dull-colored string or yarn, with stripes of one or more bright colors at the ends. The sides can be decorated with patterns or designs, if you wish, and the way in which these are woven is described later.

The use of 21 warp strings will make a bag 5 inches wide. The bag shown in Fig. 1 is square and is turned over at the top $1\frac{1}{2}$ inches. This makes $6\frac{1}{2}$ inches of weaving for each side of the bag, or a 13-inch strip altogether. Use one long piece of string for the warp and thread it on the center notches of the loom. Fasten one end of the string through the cuts in the left side of the loom. Bring the string up under the loom to notch 4 at the bottom. Pull the string under the loom and up through notch 5. Continue in this way until the 21 warp threads are in position. Fasten the end of the string in the cuts on the right side of the loom.

A flat tape needle makes a good weaving-needle. If you have difficulty getting one of these, you can make a needle of the same shape, as shown in Fig. 2, from a piece of heavy cardboard. As a rule, it is best to weave with pieces of string or yarn not more than 1 yard long. This makes the work easier, since there is not such a long piece of weft to pull across the loom as each row is made. When you come to the end of a piece of weft, tie a new piece to it with a tight square knot, and cut off all but $\frac{1}{4}$ inch of the ends of the knot. After the weaving is finished, these ends are pushed through to the wrong side.

The actual weaving is done by passing the needle carrying the weft over and under the warp strings. The first row is woven across at the top of the loom, right under the row of notches. As each succeeding row is completed, press it up tightly against the previous row. This can be done with the fingers or with a wide-toothed comb.

The end of the weft, shown at A in Fig. 2, and the corresponding end at the lower end of weaving, are fastened by weaving them back on the wrong side of the fabric. The ends that are left when you finish weaving with one color and change to another color, as when weaving the stripes in the turned-over part of the bag, are fastened in the same manner.

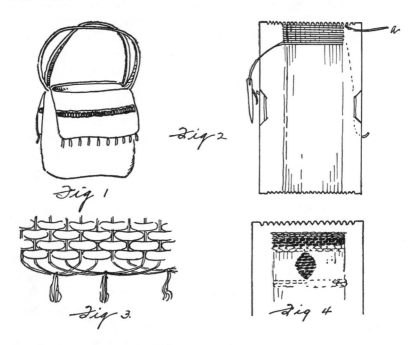

Fig 1

Fig 2

Fig 3.

Fig 4

When, in making the bag, you have finished the 13-inch strip that forms the body of the bag, cut the warp strings where they pass underneath the center of the loom. Tie these strings along the ends, as shown in Fig. 3, and then cut them off to form a short fringe, as in Fig. 1. Fold the woven strip in the middle and turn over 1½ inches on each side at the top. Sew the sides together with the same string or yarn as that used in making the bag. The handles are made either by the method described in the section on "Spool Knitting" or in the section on "Watch Chains Made of String."

It is very easy to weave simple patterns or designs on the sides of a bag, which add very greatly to its attractiveness. Draw the pattern, just the size you wish to weave it, on a piece of paper. Plan the design on quarter-inch squares, since the warp strings are $\frac{1}{4}$ inch apart. Then paste the paper to the surface of the loom at the place under the warp strings where the pattern is to be in the weaving. Do the straight-across weaving until you reach the upper edge of the design. Then, using a different color, weave the design (Fig. 4). When it is completed, the background is woven in. It is best to weave the parts of the background on each side of the design separately.

HAND-WOVEN MATS

THESE mats can be made of many colors and in numberless designs. A solid background with different colored and differently arranged stripes is always effective, or the mats can have center designs of many kinds. Some of the most interesting little mats are reproductions in miniature of Indian rugs, woven of white or gray cord with the designs done in red and black. You can make the mats any size you wish; all you have to do is to make a cardboard loom that will be large enough to hold the finished fabric. Thin, tightly twisted cord can be used, or fluffy cotton string. Experimenting with the many different kinds of string and cord that can be obtained today, is part of the fun of this kind of weaving.

The loom used for weaving mats is of the oblong cardboard type already described. In making a mat like the one shown, it is advisable to use 12 or 16 warp strings, or some other number that can be divided by four. This is done because, when the mat is finished, the warp threads are tied together to form the fringe in groups of four. Be sure to keep your rows of weaving pressed closely together as you proceed with the work, so the mat will have a firm and even texture.

When the mat has been woven to the desired size, cut the warp strings in the middle of the under side of the loom. Tie them as shown at the right of the drawing. The first two strings on the left side of one end are tied to the fifth and sixth strings; then the third and fourth strings are tied to the seventh and eighth, and so on. When all have been tied, cut them off to form an even fringe.

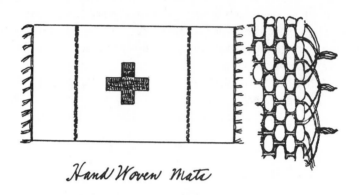

Hand Woven Mats

A DOLL'S HAMMOCK

THE doll's hammock is made on a rectangular cardboard loom of the same kind as that used for weaving mats and bags. The width of the hammock is determined by the number of warp strings, and a good width is 3 inches, which calls for the threading of thirteen warp strings, each ¼ of an inch apart. One end of the warp should be fastened through the cuts in the left side of the loom. The warp should then be threaded through the notches at each end, and should go completely around the loom; down the front, up the back, down the front again, and so on.

Any kind of string you wish to use may make up the weft. Weave it back and forth, as already explained and as shown in the various drawings, until the woven, or center part, of the hammock is about

5½ inches long. Different colored strings can be used, if you wish to have a striped hammock. When the weaving is finished, turn the loom over and cut the warp strings in the middle, on the back side of the loom. Then knot the strings together at each end and the hammock is ready to be hung between the branches of a bush or on the verandah of a doll's house.

A CIRCULAR MAT AND A TAM-O'-SHANTER

A CIRCULAR mat, woven of seine cord, jute yarn or some other kind of string, light or heavy, according to the size of the mat, is made on a circular cardboard loom such as the one shown in Fig. 1. To make the loom, draw a circle the size you wish the mat to be, on a piece of heavy cardboard. With a pencil and ruler draw two lines that divide the circle into four quarters. By drawing other lines, divide the circle into eighths, then sixteenths, and then thirty-seconds. Then cut the notches, as shown in the drawing.

Tie a knot in one end of the string you are going to use for the warp and pass it through the slit at A. Thread the loom by carrying the warp straight across the circle to notch 17, behind the tab to notch 16, across the face of the circle to notch 33, behind to notch 32, across to notch 15, and so on until the entire loom is threaded. Tie the end of the warp to the string that stretches from A to the opposite notch.

Begin weaving from the center, carrying the weft round and round, and over and under the alternate strands of the warp. Draw the first few rounds very tightly. Weave out to the edge of the circle. When you take the mat from the loom, there will be small loose loops all around the edge. These are eliminated by pulling the weaving very gradually from the center to the ends of the loops.

A mat of this kind can easily be transformed into a very becoming tam-o'-shanter for a doll. When you remove the weaving from the loom, pass a piece of string through the little loops around the out-side edge. Then, by pulling on the ends of the string, you can draw the weaving in so it will be in the shape of a tam-o'-shanter. The ends of the string are then tied together.

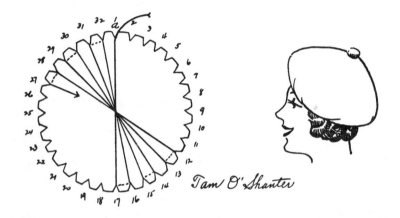

Tam O'Shanter

TABLET WEAVING

TABLET weaving, although one of the oldest forms of weaving and believed by some to be the origin of all weaving, is very little known in our country. It is still practiced by the peasants in some of the remote parts of northern and central Europe, the art having been handed down from one generation to another for no one knows how many hundreds of years. This kind of weaving is easy and interesting to do, and the method used is so different from any other that it always excites the interest of those who see it for the first time, and usually they want to try it themselves at the very first opportunity.

Tablet weaving is only suitable for making braids and bands. In early times (and even today in some parts of the East) it was used for weaving camel harness and bridles for horses and mules. By blending differently colored lengths of string, some exceptionally attractive patterns can be made.

The early tablet weavers used tablets made of thin polished wood, bone or tortoise-shell; but the kind recommended for present-day use are made from stiff cardboard. This material can be obtained by cutting it from cardboard boxes. Each tablet should measure about 2 inches square and, as shown in Fig. 1, a small hole is punched or bored about ¼ inch in from each of the four corners.

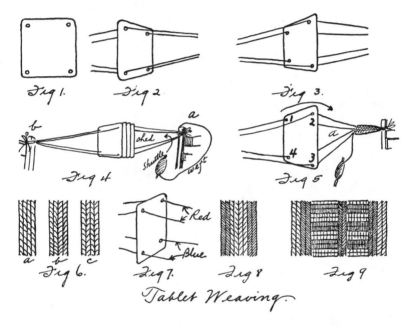

Tablet Weaving.

Four strings are used to thread each tablet, one being passed through each hole, as in Fig. 2. The length of the strings depends upon the length of the braid or band to be made. After each tablet has been threaded, the four strings are tied together at one end.

In Fig. 2 the tablet is said to be threaded left, or the warp is said to be drawn to the left. This simply means that the tablet is turned toward the left against the warp strings. In Fig. 3, on the other hand, the tablet is turned over toward the right. It is then said to be threaded right, and the warp is said to be drawn to the right.

In weaving, a number of tablets are used—four, six, eight or even more, the number of tablets determining the width of the finished fabric. The strings are all knotted at one end and are fastened over a hook, a chair, or a bed post. The other ends of the warp strings are loosely knotted and, for a short piece of weaving, fastened to the weaver's belt by a safety-pin. For a long piece of weaving, these ends can be wound around the weaver's waist. This method of handling the free ends of the warp strings has the advantage that by bending backward or forward the weaver can regulate the tension of the warp.

Another method of holding the warp in place during the weaving is to place each end of the strings over a knob on a chair, or to place one end over a bed post and the other end over a chair. (Fig 4). The left-hand end should be loosely knotted, as it will have to be untied during the weaving.

When the tablets and warp are arranged in one of these ways, wind the weft—a long piece of thin cotton string—to a small stick about the size of a pencil. This is the shuttle. Then tie the free end of the weft to the right-hand support holding the warp, as at A, Fig. 4. Pass the shuttle through the opening, or "shed," between the upper and lower warp strings and pull tight. Now you are ready to start the actual weaving.

Start with four threaded tablets. This will make a plait four strands wide. Thread the tablets all one way, say, for example, to the right (Fig. 5). Start the weaving by turning all four tablets a quarter turn to the right, as indicated by the arrow in Fig. 5. This will bring hole No. 1 in the position of hole No. 2, hole No. 2 in the position of hole No. 3, and so on. By this turn, the strings passing through holes No. 2 will be lowered, while the strings passing through holes No. 4 will be raised. Pass the shuttle through the new opening between the warp strings. Make another quarter turn with the tablets and pass the shuttle through again, pulling the weft tight.

Continue in the same way, turning the tablets in the same direction, and the warp strings will be formed into four strong twists side by side. The weft which is passed back and forth through the opening between the upper and lower warp strings, binds the twists together into a firm, ribbed fabric (Fig. 5).

It is advisable to have a beater for beating the strings up tight. This is a thin piece of wood such as a ruler or a paper knife. After each quarter-turn and the passing through of the weft, the beater is used to press or beat the weft up toward the right-hand end of the weaving.

If the tablets are all threaded the same way, the plaits will consist of a series of spiral twists all running the same way (A, Fig. 6). If, however, the tablets are threaded in pairs, two left and two right, the plait will come out as shown at B, Fig. 6. Still a third kind of plait, which is shown at C, Fig. 6, is made by threading the tablets alternately, one right, one left, one right, one left. These variations can, of course, also be used when weaving broader plaits made with more than four tablets.

As you weave and keep turning the tablets constantly in the same direction, the open working space, A in Fig. 5, will become so small that it will be impossible to turn the tablets any farther. When this happens, untie the loosely tied warp strings at B, Fig. 4, untwist them, and tie again.

Weaving Vari-Colored Patterns

A Plait with a Different Color on each Side

A two-color fabric, red on one side, for example, and blue on the other, is woven by threading the tablets as in Fig. 7 with two red and two blue strings. Arrange the tablets used, whatever their number may be, so that all the red strings are above and the blue below. Then, when weaving, turn the tablets *completely around* each time so that the red strings are always on top and the blue below.

A Striped Plait

A striped plait of two colors such as the one shown in Fig. 8 is made with eight tablets (there being eight twisted rows). Tablets 1, 2, 7 and 8 are threaded with dark-colored strings, and tablets 3, 4, 5 and 6 with light strings or strings of a contrasting color. The fabric shown in Fig. 8 is produced by threading the first four tablets, counting from the left, to the right, and threading the remaining four tablets to the left. Alternative methods of threading the tablets can, of course, be used to make other kinds of fabrics, as indicated in Fig. 6.

A large number of different designs can be woven with these fascinating sets of tablets. Each tablet, for example, can be threaded with a different color of string. Furthermore, the tablets can be turned a quarter-turn, a half-turn, or a whole turn, to bring different colors to the top and thus cause them to appear in the finished fabric.

An example of the effects that can be obtained, once one has become familiar with how to work with the tablets, is shown in Fig. 9. This plait is made with twenty tablets and is, accordingly, twenty rows wide. Tablets 1, 2, 19 and 20 have four white strings each. These form the white outside rows on the sides. Tablets 3, 4, 10, 11, 17 and 18 have four blue, red or other dark-colored strings each. These form the rows of solid color. The remaining tablets—5, 6, 7, 8, 9 and 12, 13, 14, 15, 16—have two white and two blue strings each. These give the alternating blue and white cross rows. These rows are made by handling the tablets so that the blue threads are uppermost for two weaves, then the white uppermost for two weaves. The tablets do not need to be turned all together in weaving a pattern of this kind; so many may be given a quarter-turn and so many a half-turn, according to the color that must be uppermost to make the pattern.

DAISY MATS

WEAVING these interesting little mats is different from any other kind of string work. It is weaving with a difference, and very easy and fascinating to do.

A special kind of weaving-frame is needed. It is made from pieces of wood nailed together to form a square, the dimensions of the square depending upon the size you wish the mats to be. A good size is about 8 or 10 inches to each side. The side pieces of the frame should measure about 1½ inches wide and ½ inch or 1 inch thick. When the frame has been put together, drive brads or thin nails, as shown in Fig. 1, placing them 1½ inches apart.

For weaving use heavy soft finish cotton string, which somewhat

resembles wool. The mats may be made either with white or colored
string or with several different colors as is explained below.

Fig. 1 shows how the frame is threaded. Begin at A, and when
B is reached, turn the frame so that the right-hand bottom corner, C,
becomes the left-hand bottom corner. Then continue threading as
before, and keep turning until there are ten strands each way of the
frame. The mat is then ready to be tied and cut to form the "daisies."
How this is done is described in the next paragraph in which the
method of stringing the frame to make a multi-colored mat is
explained.

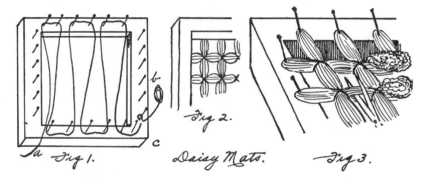

Fig. 1.   Daisy Mats.   Fig. 3.

Let us suppose that you wish to make a mat that has red, yellow,
pink, and white "daisies" on a blue background. Thread the frame
with blue string until there are three strands each way of the frame.
Finish off by tying the string to the last nail. Now thread with the
red string until there are four strands each way, then yellow for
three, pink for two, and white for one each way across the frame.

The frame is now threaded and is ready for tying. This is done
at the back of the frame with very thin twine. Fig. 2 shows how the
tying is done. The strands are tied together at each point where they
cross each other.

When the tying is completed, turn the frame over, and with a
pair of scissors cut through the strings, *except the three strands of
blue,* exactly halfway between the points where the strands cross
each other. Fig. 3 shows the mat partly cut, and two of the "daisies"
formed. When all the cuts have been made, the surface of the mat

will be almost entirely covered with regularly spaced, brightly colored round fluffy balls which are the "daisies." These can be made softer by passing a comb backward and forward through them.

When the mat is finished, it is lifted off the nails, and is ready to be wrapped up as a present for someone or to be placed on the table and put to immediate use.

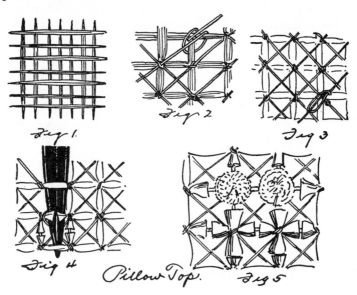

Fig 1.   Fig 2.   Fig 3

Fig 4   Pillow Top.   Fig 5

A PILLOW TOP

A GOOD-LOOKING and unusual pillow top can be made by the same method as that used in making a Daisy Mat. A wooden frame should be made of the required size, which will be determined by the size of the pillow. Drive a row of nails around the edge of the frame, spacing the nails an equal distance from one another.

No. 3 Silkine pearl cotton is good material for use for a pillow top, but soft colored strings, worsted, or even seine cord can be used. After you have decided what colors to use, put the bottom color on the frame by winding the cord around the nails, winding first from the bottom to the top and then from side to side, as in Fig. 1.

When the frame has been threaded, the "daisies" are made by clove-hitching additional strands around each intersection of the threaded strands. A strong cord should be used for this work, but one that is not too heavy. Cord known as No. 3 D.M.C., which can be purchased under this name at department stores, is recommended.

Make a clove hitch, as shown in Fig. 2, around each intersection of the threaded strands. Start at the upper left-hand corner, and run the strands from left to right at an upward 45-degree angle, repeating these strands until you reach the lower right-hand corner. Then clove-hitch a similar series of strands that run from left to right at a downward 45-degree angle. When you have finished, the work will be criss-crossed by the clove-hitched strands, as shown in Fig. 3.

It is best to make a thin, narrow stick or to use a thin paper-cutter or ruler for the next step—that of cutting the threaded strands. Insert the stick between the clove-hitched strands and the threaded strands, as shown in Fig. 4. Then, with a very sharp knife or a razor blade, cut the threaded strands between each intersection. This forms the clusters or "daisies," which are brushed up to make them fluffy (Fig. 5). Each cluster should then be pinched up with the fingers to give it its final shape.

BRAIDING

THERE are a number of different kinds of braiding—many more than most people realize—and several of the most useful and interesting types are described in the following pages. String and cord of all thicknesses and materials may be used. In many braided articles, strands of different colors are used to bring out the pattern of the braid.

Before starting a braid the ends of the strands should be fastened firmly to some stationary object so they will stay in place while the work is being done. In simple three-strand braiding, the ends of the strands are usually tied together, but in flat braiding, with a greater number of strands, it is helpful to keep the strands flat and side by side. A good way to keep strings or cords in order is to place their ends on a piece of gummed paper, fold the paper over them, and insert the paper in a paper clip or clamp. After the ends have been secured in this way, the work should be fastened to a sofa cushion with a safety-pin or placed in a vise, under a heavy book, or in a drawer which is then closed to hold the ends.

When long strands are being used, they can be kept from tangling by rolling up the greater part of each strand and securing it with a rubber band.

Three-Strand Braiding

There are two methods of plaiting a three-strand flat braid: the weaving and the alternating method. In the first the right-hand strand is carried over the middle strand and under the left-hand strand. The strand which is now on the left is then carried over and under the other two strands, and the braiding is continued in this manner until the end. This type of braid is known among sailors as English sennit.

In the alternating method of braiding, the right-hand strand is carried over the center strand, then the left-hand strand is carried over the center one, then the right-hand strand goes over the center one, and so on. This type of braiding, known among sailors as French sennit, makes a circular braid.

The alternating method can also be used with more than three strands. When making a five-strand plait, the right-hand strand is carried over one, and under one. Then the left-hand strand goes over one and under one. When you use an even number of strands such as four, the two center strands must be crossed at the beginning. The left center strand is first carried over the right center strand. The right-hand strand then goes under one and over one, and the braiding continues in this way to the end.

Three-Strand Solid Braiding

(For Watch-fobs)

In this method of braiding, the strands are held between the left thumb and forefinger and the braid is built up vertically from bottom to top. Smooth-finished twine, seine cord or shoe-laces may be used for this type of braiding.

Start by tying the ends of the three strands together and hold them between the left thumb and forefinger, as at A. Bring the front strand, No. 1, to the right over strand No. 2, but make a small loop with No. 1 and hold the loop with your thumb (B and C). Bring strand No. 2 to the left over strands Nos. 1 and 3 (D). Then pass No. 3 to the front over No. 2 and push it through the loop formed by No. 1 (E).

Three Strand Solid Braiding

Pull the three-strand tight, and you will have a triangular-shaped braid, as shown at F. Continue the braiding by repeating the steps described above. The finished work will be six-sided, as shown at G. When the braid is the length you wish it to be, cut the strands, leaving ends about one-half inch long. Using a knife or an awl, push each end into the braid under the last row of the work.

Four-Strand Spiral Braiding

(For Watch-fobs, Children's Reins, Curtain Pulls, etc.)

This makes a very good-looking braid which can be used for a watch-fob, a curtain pull or for children's reins. Start by tying the ends of the four strands together and hold the ends between the left thumb and forefinger, as at A.

Begin by passing the front strand, No. 1, over the right strand, No. 2, making a small loop with No. 1 as at B, which is held under the left thumb. Pass the right strand, No. 2, over both strand No. 1 and strand No. 3, so it lies between Nos. 3 and 4, as at C.

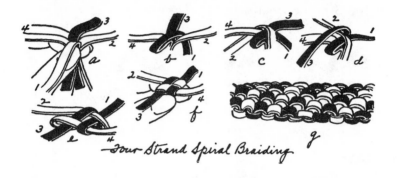

Four-Strand Spiral Braiding

Now bring the back strand, No. 3, over Nos. 2 and 4, so it lies between strand No. 4 and the loop formed by strand No. 1 (D). Then bring strand No. 4 over No. 3 and pass it through the loop. Draw all the strands tight and you will have a square as shown in F. Continue the work by repeating the steps described above. The finished work, which has a spiral running across the braid from the upper left to the lower right side, is shown at G.

Four-Strand Square Braiding

Tie the ends of the four strands together with a piece of string and hold them between the left thumb, as at A. Then start exactly as in spiral braiding and make the first square (B).

Hold the square with any side toward you. Pass the front strand across the top of the square to the back, and bring the back strand across the top to the front (C). Then weave the right-hand strand over and under these two strands, and follow by weaving the left-hand strand over and under the front and back strands (D). Draw the strands tight and the work will appear as shown at E.

Four Strand Square Braiding

The work is continued in the same way, two opposite strands being laid across the top each time, and the two remaining strands being woven through them. The finished braid is shown at F. The work is finished off by cutting the ends of the strands off short and tucking them under the last row of the braiding.

Four-Strand Round Braiding

(For Girdles, Whistle Lanyards, Hat Cords, Plate Mats, Coasters, Children's Reins)

This type of braiding can be used for making a number of articles such as girdles, whistle lanyards, and hat cords. It is also an excellent braid to use for plate mats and coasters for glasses. When used for this purpose, the braid is coiled up to form a circular mat, and the adjoining rows are sewed together. The sewing should be done on a flat table top so the braids can be pressed down and kept even, and in flat rows.

The preliminary arrangement of the strands is shown at A. The ends of the strands should be fastened to some stationary object so their order will not be disarranged. Fastening them in a paper clamp is recommended. It is also a help to arrange them around a short piece of cardboard, which helps to keep them in place. The cardboard is removed as soon as the work is well under way.

Start by bringing the second strand from the left, No. 2, across No. 3. Then pass No. 1 under No. 3. Bring No. 4 over No. 2 and under No. 1.

Commence to braid by bringing the upper left-hand strand, No. 3, across the back and bring it out between strands Nos. 2 and 1.

Cross it over No. 1 and bring it back to the left next to No. 4, as at B. Then pass the upper right-hand strand, No. 2, across the back and bring it out between No. 4 and No. 3. Cross it over No. 3 and bring it back to the right next to No. 1, as at C.

Now pass the upper left-hand strand, No. 4, across the back and bring it out between Nos 1 and 2. Cross it over No. 2 and back to the left, as at D. Then pull the work up tight.

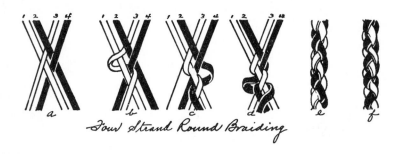

Four Strand Round Braiding

Continue as follows: Pass the upper right-hand strand across the back; bring it out between the two left-hand strands; cross it over the lower strand and bring it back to the right. Pass the upper left-hand strand across the back; bring it out between the two right-hand strands; cross it over the lower strand and bring it back to the left. The work continues in the same way until the braid is as long as you want it to be.

Two different patterns that can be made by arranging strands of contrasting colors in different order are shown at E and F. In braid E, the strands are arranged in alternate colors—No. 1 light, No. 2 dark, No. 3 light, and No. 4 dark. In braid F the strands are arranged so the two of the same color are together; that is, Nos. 1 and 2 light, and Nos. 3 and 4 dark.

Four-Strand Braiding Over Double Strands

(For Braided Sandals, Hat Bands, Belts, Book Marks)

In braiding, the working strand may be carried over or under two adjacent strands, instead of over and under single strands. This method adds strength to the braid, and for this reason it is recommended for making such articles as the braided jute yarn sandals described below.

The method of braiding with four strands over double strands is illustrated above. The outer left-hand strand, No. 1, is brought over both No. 2 and No. 3, so that No. 1 is next to No. 4. The outer right-hand strand, No. 4, is then brought over No. 1, so it is next to No. 3. Continue by bringing the outer left-hand strand over both the strand on its right and the next strand also; then bring the outer right-hand strand over one strand at its left. The completed braid resembles regular three-strand braiding, but the left-hand edge is thicker than the right.

Flat Braiding with Five or More Strands

(For Book Marks, Belts, Hat Bands, etc.)

The method of making a five-strand flat braid with smooth-finished twine is illustrated opposite. The strands may be of two or more contrasting colors, and many variegated designs can be obtained by arranging the colors in different orders.

In five-strand braiding, start by bringing the outer left-hand strand, No. 1, over No. 2, so that No. 1 is next to No. 3. Then bring the outer right-hand strand, No. 5, over No. 4, under No. 3, and over

No. 1, so that No. 5 is next to No. 2. Continue by repeating the following two steps: (1) bring the outer left-hand strand over the strand at its right; then (2) bring the outer right-hand strand over the strand at its left, under the next strand, and over the next one.

This same method of braiding can be used with a greater number of strands. The first step—bringing the outer left-hand strand over the strand at its right—is always the same. The second step differs according to the number of strands. If there is an *odd* number of strands, the outer right-hand strand is passed *over* the strand at its left. If there is an *even* number of strands, the outer right-hand strand is passed *under* the strand at its left.

Eight-Strand Round Braiding

(For Watch-fobs, Girdles, Hat Cords, Childrens' Reins, Dog Leashes, Braided Rugs)

The method of arranging the strands and the kind of braid produced by eight-strand round braiding are shown on page 126. Before commencing to braid, the ends of the strands should be secured so the strands will stay in their proper order. They may be pinned to a sofa cushion or may be placed on a strip of gummed paper, the paper folded over them, and the ends held in place by a paper clip or clamp.

To arrange the strands as shown at A, Pass No. 4 over No. 5, under No. 6, over No. 7, and under No. 8. Then pass strands Nos. 3, 2, and 1 over and under Nos. 5, 6, 7, and 8 (alternately).

Begin the braiding with the upper right-hand strand, No. 4. Pass No. 4 across the back and bring it out at the left between the second and third strands from the bottom, Nos. 6 and 7. Pass it over No. 7, and under No. 8, and then back to the right (B). Next pass the upper left-hand strand, No. 5, across the back, and bring it out at the right between the second and third strands from the bottom, Nos. 2 and 1. Pass it over No. 1 and under No. 4 and back to the left (C).

Eight Strand Round Braiding

Continue the braiding in the same way. Pull the work up tight each time that you bring a working strand back to the side from which it started. The finished braid is shown at D.

Round Braiding Over a Band

If you are making a bracelet, ring, or some other article on which the braiding is made around a band, each length of the string or cord used as braiding material should be long enough to make two strands when it is passed around the band. Below is shown at A two cords making four strands on the front of a band. The arrangements for six and eight strands are shown at B and C.

BRAIDED BRACELETS AND RINGS

UNUSUAL bracelets can be made of brightly colored cords braided over metal bands. The bands may be of sheet brass or sheet copper, either of which may be obtained at any hardware store. They are cut to the desired size with metal shears. For a child's bracelet, the band should be about 9 inches long; for a medium-sized hand 10 inches long.

The ends of the band are joined together by interlocking two V-shaped cuts, each about ½ inch from one end of the band, as shown in Fig. 1. When the cuts have been interlocked, the bracelet is put over some solid object and the ends are hammered flat with a mallet.

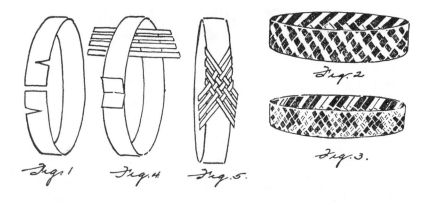

The strings are braided around the band by the method described under "Round Braiding Over a Band." Four lengths of cord are needed, each about 80 inches long. Two colors are used, which can be arranged in different ways to produce different patterns. Since the cords are doubled in the center, you will have four strands to work with.

If the cords are arranged so the colors alternate, the design will be a diagonal one, as shown in Fig. 2. Two cords of one color followed by two cords of the contrasting color will give alternating diamond shapes, as in Fig. 3. Three strands of one color followed by one strand of a contrasting color will produce broader diamond shapes of the first color.

Start the braiding by placing the centers of the four strands across the inside of the bracelet an inch or so away from the joined ends, as shown in Fig. 4. Hold the strands in place between the thumb and fingers of the left hand, and braid the four right-hand strands through the four left-hand strands, as shown in Fig. 5. Pull the braids up tight so they will lie flat.

Begin the braiding with the upper right-hand strand. Pass this strand across the inside of the bracelet, bring it out at the left between the third and second strands from the bottom, then bring it over the second strand and under the first strand, back to the right. Then pass the upper left-hand strand across the inside of the bracelet, bring it out between the second and third strands at the right, over the second, under the first, and back to the left.

The work is continued in the same way, first using the upper right-hand strand, and then the upper left-hand strand. When you have worked all the way around the bracelet, the pattern must be completed and the ends tucked out of sight. There will be four strands on each side which will be in the same order as at the start. The first, second and third of the right-hand strands will be found to come out to the edge of the bracelet, while the first and second of the left-hand strands will be found to come out to the edge.

Cut off the ends of the strands diagonally to give them points. Then, with an awl, loosen up the first three strands of the braiding, made at the beginning. Work the fourth strand on the right-hand side under the first strand on the same side, so it will come out at the right-hand edge. Next pass the third strand on the left-hand side over the adjoining strand and work it under one strand and out to the left-hand edge. Pass the fourth strand on the left-hand side over one and work it under one and out to the left-hand edge. All four strands on each side will now be out to the edge of the bracelet.

The work is now finished off inside the bracelet. First loosen the first two diagonal strands made at the beginning on the inside of the bracelet. Do not loosen the straight strands, as the work passes over them. Pass the first strand on the left inside the bracelet and work it up under the two diagonal strands on the right. Bring it out to the edge, but do not pull it tight. Work the first strand at the right under the strand you have just made and the strand next above it, and bring it out to the edge. Continue in the same way, first with the left-hand and then with the right-hand strands, working each strand under two diagonal strands and out to the edge. When all the strands have been worked into place, pull the work up tight and cut the ends of the strands off close to the edges of the bracelet.

Finger rings can be made in the same way as bracelets, by using very fine string or heavy silk or cotton thread.

A BRAIDED DOG LEASH

FOR the braided dog leash shown below, you will need 4 lengths of stout smooth-finished twine or seine cord, each 3½ yards long, a rope core about ⅛-inch thick and 1¾ yards long, and a good strong clasp or snap. The four braiding strands should preferably be of two colors.

Locate the center of the rope core, which will be 31½ inches from either end, and the centers of the four strands, 63 inches from the ends. Place the strands along the core with their centers at the center of the core and tie the strands to the core at the center points with a short piece of string.

Now measure 15 inches from one end of the core and turn that end back to the 15-inch point to make the loop by which the leash is to be held. Bind the end tightly to the standing part of the leash with a piece of strong thin cord or fish-line. Have this binding about 1 inch long.

Fasten the work to some stationary object by means of the string by which the strands and the core are tied together. Arrange the work so the handle loop is toward you.

The braiding is to be started where the strands are tied to the center of the core. Arrange the strands for four-strand round braiding. It is helpful to insert a little strip of cardboard over the core and to keep it in place until the first row of braiding has been completed. The cardboard is then removed and the work is continued with round braiding, the working strands being passed from the upper left or right, behind the core and up on the opposite side. The work should be pulled up tight each time the working strand is brought back to its original side.

When the braiding comes to the point where the loop is bound to the standing part, continue the round braiding right over the join, on around the loop, and back to within about ½ inch of the join. For the next two or three rows of work, make the round braiding around both sides of the loop. Then hold the loop downward in your left hand and work a spiral braid one inch or more in length in order to reinforce the join. End this part of the work by passing the ends back under the last row of braiding, and cut off the ends of the strands, leaving them about ¾ of an inch long.

Now measure off 5 inches from the opposite end of the core. Slip the clasp over this end and turn the end back to the 5-inch point. Then bind the end to the standing part with a piece of strong thin cord or fish-line, making the binding about 1 inch long.

Untie the string that was used to fasten the strands to the core at their center points and tie it around the finished braiding 3 or 4 inches back from the center. Then fasten the looped end to some stationary object (it may be looped over a bed post) so the unfinished end of the core is toward you. Cover the remaining half of the core with round braiding in the same manner as the first half. The join at the clasp end is covered in the same way as the join at the end of the loop handle, and the work is finished off by passing the ends under the last row of the braiding and cutting off the ends, leaving them about ¾ of an inch long.

A BRAIDED WHISTLE LANYARD

(Made with Four-strand Round Braiding and Spiral Braiding.)

THIS lanyard is made so that one end of the loop, which goes around the user's neck, will slide up and down the standing part or free end of the lanyard. When you have made one, all your friends will be wanting to know how you did it.

Cut two lengths of seine cord or stout smooth-finished twine, each 3½ yards long. Pass the cords through the ring of a spring clip of the type shown above, and draw them through until the clip is at the center of the cords. The two cords will then form four strands of equal length. Arrange the strands for four-strand round braiding, secure the ends of the strands to some stationary object, and work four-strand round braiding until you come to a point within 12 inches of the ends of the strands. The braided length will then be about 40 inches long.

Remove the work from the stationary object to which it is fastened. Make a long loop by putting the end of the braided part against some point on the standing part of the braided part. The remaining 12 inches of the strands are now to be spirally braided around the standing part as a core. This makes the sleeve which permits the loop to move up and down the standing part.

When making the sleeve, hold the lanyard between your left thumb and forefinger, with the loop downward. If you are using two colors, arrange the strands so the front and back strands are of one color and the right and left strands of the other color.

Start by making one row of spiral braiding right around the core. Draw it up firmly, but not too tight. Continue by doing spiral braiding until the sleeve or collar is 1 inch long. The sleeve must be firmly braided, but not pulled up so tight that the core or standing part of the lanyard cannot move through it freely. Finish off the spiral braiding by pushing the ends of the strands under the last row of the work. Then cut off the ends, leaving them about 1 inch long, so there will be no danger of their slipping out of place.

BRAIDED JUTE YARN SANDALS

FOR a pair of size 6 sandals of the kind shown on page 132, you will need 4 lengths of jute yarn each about 21 feet long. Two lengths are used for each sandal. You will also need a pair of inner soles which you can buy at a shoe or department store. Tie two lengths of the jute yarn together at their center points with a piece of string and fasten the string to a hook driven into the wall, a table leg, or some other stationary object. Double the two lengths so you have four strands, each about 10½ feet long. Then braid the lengths by the four-strand braiding method described on page 124 (Four Strand Braiding Over Double Strands). When the braid is finished, it will be about 8 feet long. The braiding should be firm, but should not be pulled too tight.

The next step is to sew the braid to one of the inner soles. The soles should be of material soft enough to sew through and should be about ½ inch narrower than the width of the completed sandal. First sew the braid on the bottom of the sole, using linen thread. Start at the instep and sew the braid on flat around the edge, allowing it to project about the thickness of one strand beyond the edge. Sew through the sole, and keep the stitches in line, so they will sink into the braiding and be concealed. Continue sewing the braid to the sole, placing the rows very close together, until you come to the center of the sole. At the center you will probably have to pull the braid to spread it out a little in order to fill the center space. Cut the braid, leaving a short end which can be worked under the inner row of braiding. Spreading the ends apart, insert them under the preceding row, and sew them down as flat as possible. You will probably have to cut one or two stitches of the preceding row to make room for the spread-out end strands.

Now turn the sole over and sew the braid to the top in the same way.

The straps are made of two strips of braid cut to the required length. One end of each strap is inserted at the side of the heel. Cut one or two stitches in the outer row of braiding at these points, spread the end strands of the straps flat, insert them beneath the outer row of braid, and sew them to the sole. Each strap is sewed around the heel and is then carried across the sandal to a point near the tip of the sandal, where the free end is inserted beneath the outer row of braiding and sewed in place. The two straps cross at the back of the sandal and form a grip for the heel. The straps are sewed together at the point where they cross each other. A heel strap may be added, as shown in the illustration, if desired. When the straps are in place, sew all the way around the edge of the sandal to hold the braids on the top and bottom of the sandal firmly together.

RUGS MADE OF BRAIDED JUTE YARN

JUTE yarn is a loosely twisted but sturdy form of twine which can be obtained at department and hardware stores and many of the larger stationery stores. It comes in a wide range of colors and provides a splendid medium for making rugs that are decorative as well as useful. These rugs are principally used for porches and for such houses as country cottages; but they can also be used in the bedrooms of city houses.

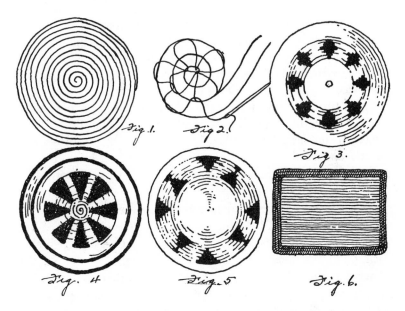

Fig. 1.   Fig 2.   Fig 3.   Fig. 4   Fig. 5   Fig. 6.

Braided rugs are made of one or more plaited or braided strands, in this instance, made of jute yarn or twine, though other materials such as colored pieces of cloth are also used. When jute yarn is used, three pieces or strands are usually combined to form each strand used for plaiting. Three such strands are then braided together to make the plait or plaits of which the rug is made. All three strands (consisting of three lengths of jute yarn apiece) may be the same color, or may be of different colors. Much of the fun of making rugs of this kind is in experimenting with different color combinations in the braiding. Four-strand braiding may also be used.

Whatever the number of strands used in a braid, they should never be very long or else they will get tangled up and become difficult to handle. Lengths from 1 to 1½ yards are best. Join the ends of two pieces of yarn together by sewing, when one piece has been braided as far as possible, so there will be a neat, smooth join.

Circular Rugs: One of the most decorative kinds of braided rug to make is the circular rug. It is made by coiling a long strip of braid as shown in Fig. 1, the coils being held together by sewing. Strong thread, such as carpet thread, should be used for the sewing.

When sewing the coils together, start as soon as the first coil has been made. Pass the needle through the end of the braid and through the part of the first coil that lies directly beside it. Then pass the needle back through the outer coil into and through the inner piece, as in Fig. 2. Do the work on a table so you can lay the rug on the table and press it smooth as the sewing progresses. If this is not done, the rug will not lie flat when it is completed. When you have made the rug the desired size, the end of the braid is sewed to the outer coil of the rug. It can be tapered down by cutting with a pair of scissors and pressed flat, so the end will not protrude and spoil the symmetry of the rug.

Circular rugs can be made of a continuous piece of braid of the same color or colors or, by using lengths of differently colored braid, can be made in designs. Some typical Indian designs which are pleasing and effective are illustrated in Figures 3, 4, and 5. When it is necessary to change from one color to another, the new differently colored piece of braid is sewed to the end of the previous piece. This is quite difficult work and requires a good deal of time and care, but if you find that rug-making is one of the things you really like to do, this will not be any deterrent.

Still another kind of circular rug can be made by using strips or rows of alternating or contrasting colored braid. Such a rug is started with a short strip of braid just long enough to form a ring with practically no opening in the center, or else long enough to be coiled twice. Each succeeding row is sewed to the one before it, and its own two ends are carefully sewed together. Each strip of braid grows longer as the circumference of the rug increases.

Rectangular Rugs: Rectangular rugs are easier to make than the circular kind and are probably the type that most beginners will wish to start out with. They are made of a number of strips of braid—either all one color or of contrasting colors—sewed together. The strips may run either crosswise of the rug or lengthwise, usually the latter. A common method of making such a rug is to have the field or center portion all one color, and then to sew several strips of three-strand braid of a darker contrasting color around the field to serve as a border (Figure 6).

STRING GAMES AND FIGURES

THE playing of string games and the making of string figures by weaving on the hands a single loop of string, has become a favorite pastime with many thousands of people, young and old, in England; but there are very few in America who are acquainted with this absorbing and fascinating kind of game.

Most of us, of course, know how to make "Cat's Cradles," although, like our national anthem, few of us can carry it through to the end, a complicated and difficult proceeding. Cat's Cradles is probably one of the most widely played games in all the world. It is well known in China, Japan, Korea, Borneo, Australia, the Philippine Islands, and hundreds of other Pacific Ocean island groups. It is believed that it originated in one of the countries of the Far East many hundreds of years ago. It is one of the favorite pastimes of the Eskimos. In some regions they play the game most often when the sun is going south in the fall, their hope being that they can catch the sun in the meshes of the string and prevent its disappearance. In other regions young boys are not allowed to play Cat's Cradles, because in later life their fingers might become entangled in the harpoon-line while hunting seal.

Two people and one loop of string are needed to play the game. The players alternately take the string off each other's hands to produce eight different figures, which are known as: Cradle, Soldier's Bed, Candles, Manger, Diamonds, Cat's Eye, Fish in a Dish and Clock.

"Cat's Cradles," however, is only one of many hundreds of string games or figures. The making of string figures is one of the oldest of the arts, the most universal of games, among the primitive peoples of the world. It is from them that we obtained the game of "Cat's Cradles"; and from them came all the other intriguing string pastimes described in the following pages.

"Go where you will," writes Kathleen Haddon, who has spent many years in delving into the origin of string games, "go where you will—to the arctic north or to the coral islands of the Pacific—string games are there. The Eskimos with their long winter darkness, lasting for months, have plenty of time for games and are very clever at making string pictures, many of which have chants or stories attaching to them. They will show you pictures of caribou, bears, and other animals; of birds, kayaks (skin boats), sledges and such like. Further south the American Indians, the Navaho and Apaches, who live on the clear starry plateaux of the south-western United States, will show you stars of many sorts, storms, tipis (tents) and little animals like coyotes and rabbits.

"In New Guinea you will find string pictures of headhunters, spears, drums, canoes, palm-trees, fishes and crabs. Each race has its own string figures, and when you come to think of it this is natural —for how could an Eskimo make a string picture of a palm-tree or an Australian one of a polar bear? So, by learning his string figures, you can also learn something of a native's mind—what he sees, the things he lives amongst and the things he makes—for naturally his string figures picture the things he knows best and is most familiar with."

Some natives have stories that they tell as they play their different string games, and some illustrate the old tribal legends by pictures made in string. Many of the Eskimos believe that there is a "Spirit of Cat's Cradles" which can get into its power anyone who spends too much time playing this game. This spirit is invisible, but when it comes into a hut a crackling sound is heard, like something giving off electric sparks. Then what an exciting scene ensues! The Eskimo seizes his string and starts to do the opening figure as fast as he can over and over again, for he knows that the spirit is doing the same thing and trying to do it with the speed of lightning. No one knows what might happen if the spirit ever won this race; but it would be something dreadful, of that the Eskimos are certain. Fortunately for us, the "Spirit of Cat's Cradles" lives far away in the icy north, so we need never keep one ear open to listen for that mysterious crackling sound while we are amusing ourselves with string games or making string figures.

GENERAL INSTRUCTIONS

THE string used for playing string games should be stout yet pliable; not the soft kind of string that kinks easily. A good length is about 40 inches, which will make a loop over the hands about 16 inches long. One way that is used to determine the right length for your particular size is to wrap the string eight times around the knuckles. This gives the right length without allowing for the knot. The knot should not be a big, awkward one, but as small as possible. A reef or square knot is quite all right, although some of the experts go the length of splicing the ends of the string together.

In the directions that follow the fingers are named "thumb, fore, middle, ring, and little fingers," instead of being numbered. When making string figures, the string lies around the fingers in such a way that one part of it is nearer the player and one further away. These parts are called respectively the "near" and "far" strings. When a part of the string lies across the palm of one of the hands, it is called the "palm" string. When making the figures, a finger may be passed either *under* or *over* a string, and the instructions in this respect must be carefully followed.

The majority of the figures begin in the same way, with "Position 1" or "Opening A," the latter being made from the former.

"Position 1" is made by placing the string over both little fingers and both thumbs and drawing the hands apart, as in Fig. 1.

To make "Opening A" from "Position 1," put the right forefinger under the left palm string and draw that string out as far as possible. Then put the left forefinger under the right palm string, in between the strings of the right forefinger loop, and draw the left hand back as far as it will go. When the hands are drawn apart, the strings will be arranged as shown in Fig. 2.

When a loop is transferred from one finger to another, it must not be twisted. For example, the near string of the loop must remain on the near side and the far string on the far side.

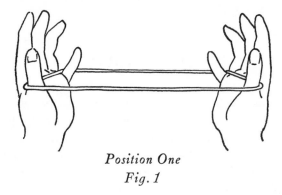

Position One
Fig. 1

The strings should be kept near the tips of the fingers, particularly at the end of a figure when the fingers are extended and the figure displayed. However, a *new* loop picked up by a finger which already has a loop upon it must always be kept *above* the original loop; that is, nearer to the tip of the finger.

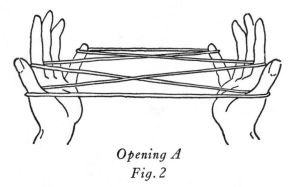

Opening A
Fig. 2

The position normally held by the hands is with the fingers pointing upward and the palms facing each other. It is usual to return to this position after each movement.

Sometimes, at first reading, the descriptions of how to make the figures may seem rather long and complicated, but they must be so in order to make the movements clear. Have a little patience, and you will soon be doing your favorite figures like lightning.

Descriptions of how to make some of the easiest, and yet most interesting, string figures are given in the following pages.

A FISH SPEAR

THE Fish Spear starts with Position 1.

With the right forefinger pick up from below the left palm string. Draw the hands apart and as you do so, twist this string down away from you and up toward you by revolving the right forefinger.

With the left forefinger pick up from below the right palm string, being sure to pick it up between the strings of the right forefinger loop and near the right forefinger where the loop is not twisted. Do not twist the right palm string as you draw the hands apart.

Release the loops from the right thumb and little finger and draw the string tight.

This represents a spear with several prongs such as is used for spearing fish by the natives in the Pacific Islands and by the Indians. The figure is a favorite with the natives of Murray Island, Torres Straits, and with the Indians of British Columbia.

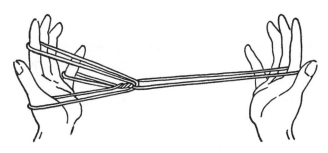

AN OUTRIGGER CANOE

START with Opening A.

Pass the two thumbs over the near forefinger strings and pick up on them the far forefinger strings from below. Bring the thumbs back to their original position.

With your teeth lift off the thumbs their original near string, leaving on the thumbs the loops just picked up.

Release the loops on the little fingers and draw the hands apart.

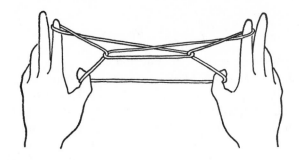

The figure, which comes from New Caledonia, represents a native canoe with an outrigger attached to one side. An outrigger is a long piece of wood fastened to the canoe by two beams. Its purpose is to keep the canoe from capsizing.

MAN ON A BED

START with Opening A.

Pass each thumb away from you under the forefinger loops and into the little finger loops from below. Pick up on the back of each thumb the near little finger strings. Bring the thumbs back under the forefinger loops to their original positions.

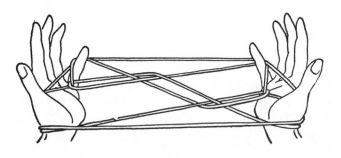

Bring the little fingers toward you. Pass them over the far fore-finger strings and under the near forefinger strings. Pick up from below on the back of the little fingers the far thumb strings and return the little fingers to position.

Release the loops on the forefingers, and you will have the man on a bed, a Torres Straits figure. Sing, "Man on a bed, man on a bed, lies asleep, lies asleep, bed breaks." On the last word release the loops from the little fingers and the bed will tumble down. The native words of the little song are "Le sikge, le sikge, uteidi, uteidi, sik erapei."

CARRYING WOOD

START with Opening A.

Put the tips of the thumb and forefinger of each hand together. Pass the joined thumbs and forefingers away from you over the fore-finger loops and into the little finger loops from below. Pick up the near little finger strings on the barks of the thumbs and return thumbs and forefingers to their original positions.

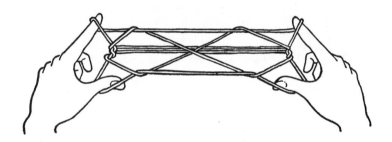

Release the loops from the little fingers.

Lift the lower loops off the thumbs and forefingers, bringing them up over the loops just picked up. Do not draw the hands apart to tighten the string. The thumb loops are most easily removed by the teeth; the forefinger loops are readily removed by picking them up between the thumb and forefinger of the opposite hand.

Now pick out the loop just released from the thumbs. Bend down the two thumbs away from you and press them against the upper string of this loop. This string is easy to pick out because it is the only free string running straight across the figure. Let the original thumb loops slip off and extend the figure between the thumbs and forefingers, turning the palms so they face away from you.

This is a Navaho Indian figure and shows the way they carry wood by means of a band that passes over their foreheads. The two central strings represent the band; the other strings represent the wood that is being carried.

THE CARIBOU

THIS is an interesting figure which, when completed, shows a caribou, with antlers facing the left hand. It comes from the Eskimos of Cumberland Sound, in Baffin Land.

The figure starts with Opening A.

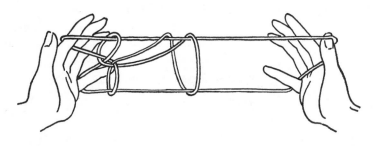

Bend the right forefinger away from you over all the strings and down on the far side of the right far little finger string. Draw the right forefinger toward you. On its near side there are both right little finger strings and the far right forefinger string. Allow the near right forefinger string to slip over the knuckle and to the far side of the forefinger.

Now put the right forefinger, still bent and holding the strings on its near side, from below into the right thumb loop. Bend the right forefinger down toward you over the near right thumb string, picking this string up on the tip of the right forefinger. Pass the forefinger away from you under all the strings and return it to its original position.

Release the loop from the right thumb.

Give the loops on the right forefinger a twist by turning the forefinger away from you, down on the near side of the little finger loop and then up toward you.

Pass the right thumb from below into the two loops on the right forefinger and draw the thumb away from the forefinger to widen the loops.

Take the loop on the left forefinger between the tips of the left thumb and forefinger. Bring this loop to the right over all the strings and pass it from above into the center of the loops passing around the right thumb and forefinger. Pass it down through these loops and then away from you. Bring it up again, without twisting it, on the near side of the right little finger loop and put it back on the left forefinger.

Release the loop from the left thumb, and release the loops passing around the right thumb and forefinger. Draw the hands slightly apart. Put the left thumb into the left little finger loop, withdrawing the right little finger. Put the right thumb and forefinger into the right little finger loop, withdrawing the right little finger. Extend the figure between the stretched apart thumbs and forefingers.

It requires a little imagination to make out the caribou; but it is as good a picture as it is possible to make with no more drawing materials than a piece of string.

AN ESKIMO HOUSE AND TWO ESKIMOS
RUNNING AWAY

THIS figure, which has a surprise ending, commences with Opening A.

Turn the palms of each hand toward you and close the four fingers of each hand over all the strings except the near thumb string. Throw this string over the backs of the hands and return to their usual position.

You now have a large loop surrounding your two hands, its strings passing across the back of each hand. On the near side of your hands, the near strings cross to form an X. Pass your thumbs away from you, putting one on each side of the point where these strings cross to form the X. Pass the thumbs under all the other strings. Then, with their backs, pick up the far string of the loop around the hands. Bring this string back toward you, carried by the thumbs. Bring the thumbs back through the sides of the X, along the same path followed on their journey away from you.

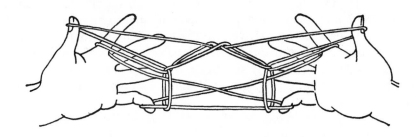

Lift the loops off the backs of the hands, passing them from back to front over the fingertips, and letting them rest on the other strings between the hands. Then draw the hands apart and you will have the Eskimo House.

At each corner of the house there stands an Eskimo man. All of a sudden a polar bear appears. They are terribly frightened and immediately run away as fast as they can, one to the left and one to the right. Let go the loops on the forefingers and draw the hands apart and you will see the two little men running away.

THE TERN

THIS is a figure devised by the natives of Murray Island, Torres Straits, and represents one of the birds found in that region. When completed, the bird can be made to come to life and flap its wings.

Start with Opening A.

Hold down the far little finger string with your foot or with a book, or some other object placed on a table.

Bring the little fingers toward you and pass them under the far forefinger strings, thus picking these strings up on the backs of the little fingers. Then pass each little finger under its respective side of the far string, held down by the foot, so that this string slips over the little fingers.

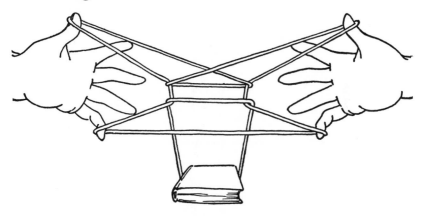

Take the near thumb string between the teeth.

Pass the thumbs under the near forefinger strings, thus picking them up. Then pass each thumb under its respective near string— held by the teeth—so that this string slips over the thumbs.

Release the strings around the forefingers and the string held by the teeth.

Hold the palms facing each other with thumbs upward, then turn the palms downward. Repeat this movement and the strings will imitate the flapping of the tern's wings, which are the loops around the little fingers.

A MAN CLIMBING A TREE

THIS is a very amusing and realistic moving figure which comes from Australia. It is very easy to make.

Start with Opening A.

Bring the little fingers toward you over the forefinger loops and into the thumb loops from above. Pick up the near thumb string on the backs of the little fingers and return them to their original positions. With the teeth or the thumb and forefinger of each hand, lift off the little fingers their original far string, passing this string over the loops just picked up, which remain on the little fingers.

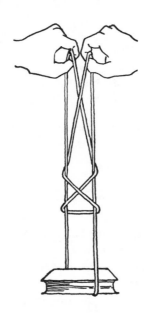

Bend the forefingers down into their own loops, thus bringing in against the palms the strings crossing the forefinger loops. The loops just released from the little fingers must be kept on the far side of the forefinger loops.

Now, with the foot or with a book on a table, hold down the far little finger string.

Release all the finger and thumb strings except those held by the forefingers against the palms.

Draw the hands slowly upwards and the man will climb the tree.

The diamond-shaped upper portion of the figure is the man's body, while the lower triangular parts are his legs wrapped around the tree trunk. As the hands move upward, the tree grows taller and taller. The man keeps climbing and finally reaches the top, where he is so high up he can hardly be seen from the ground below.

AN APACHE DOOR

THIS figure represents the decorated flap which serves as a door to the Apache Indians' tents or tepees. It is a beautifully symmetrical figure and not at all difficult to make.

Start with Opening A.

With the right thumb and forefinger pick up the left near forefinger string close to the finger. Lift the loop entirely off the left forefinger; then put the loop over the left hand and let it drop down on the left wrist. With the left thumb and forefinger pick up the right near forefinger string in the same manner. Lift the loop entirely off the right forefinger; put it over the right hand and let the loop drop down on the right wrist. Draw the strings tight by separating the hands.

With the right thumb and forefinger pick up the left near little finger string, close to the little finger. Draw this string toward you and pass it between the left forefinger and thumb; then release it. With the right thumb and forefinger pick up the left far thumb string close to the left thumb. Draw this string away from you and pass it between the left ring and little fingers; then release it.

With the left thumb and forefinger pick up the right near little finger string close to the right little finger. Draw it toward you, pass it between the right forefinger and thumb, and release it. With the left thumb and forefinger pick up the right far thumb string close to the right thumb. Draw this string away from you, pass it between the right ring and little fingers, and release it.

Keep all the loops in position on both hands during the following movements.

With the left thumb and fingers grasp all the strings where they cross in the center of the figure and pass them from left to right between the right forefinger and thumb and around the back of the thumb as far as possible. Put these strings below the double loop already on the thumb. Then, with the left thumb and forefinger, take hold of the double loop already on the right thumb and draw it over the tip of the thumb. Still holding this double loop, let the group of strings lying between the forefinger and thumb slip over the tip of the thumb. Replace the double loop on the thumb. Draw the strings tight by separating the hands.

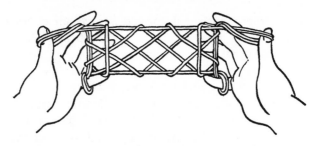

Repeat the movement on the left hand as follows: Grasp all the strings where they cross in the center of the figure with the right thumb and fingers and pass them from right to left between the left forefinger and thumb. Then with the right thumb and forefinger take hold of the double loop already on the left thumb and draw it over the tip of the thumb. Keeping tight hold of this double loop, let the group of strings lying between the left forefinger and thumb slip over the tip of the thumb. Replace the double loop on the thumb, and separate the hands to draw the strings tight.

Now lift the loops surrounding each wrist over the tips of the fingers of each hand from back to front, letting them lie on the strings between the hands.

At this point the Indians always rub the palms of their hands together, and you may do so too. This is only for effect, however, to prepare the way for the extension of the completed figure. The "door" is drawn out into shape by separating the hands.

THE FIGHTING HEADHUNTERS

THESE wild headhunters are from the Torres Straits, north of Australia. One is from Murray Island and the other from Dauar

Island. Since the figure was invented by the people of Murray Island, the Dauar Island headhunter is always vanquished in the fight, and the Murray Island man runs off home with his head.

Start the figure with Opening A. It is well to use a stiff, quite thick string, as that will make the headhunters stand up more rigidly after they have been twisted into shape.

Pass the little fingers toward you over the forefinger loops and into the thumb loops from above. With their backs pick up the near thumb string. Return the little fingers to their original positions, taking the thumb loop entirely off the thumb.

Release the thumbs.

Pass the thumbs away from you under the forefinger loops and into the little finger loops from below. On their backs pick up both near little finger strings, and return the thumbs to their original positions. Release the little fingers.

Pass the little fingers toward you over the forefinger loops and into the thumb loops from below. Pick up on their backs both far thumb strings, and return the little fingers to their original positions.

There is now a small triangle in the center of the figure. Insert the two forefingers into this from below, and, pulling out the sides of the triangle on the backs of the forefingers, separate the hands. With the teeth or with the thumb and forefinger of each hand lift off each forefinger the lower single loop surrounding it. Bring these loops up over the double loops on the forefingers and over the tips of the fingers to the palm side of the hand.

Release the thumbs, draw the strings tight, and twist the forefinger loops three times by rotating each forefinger away from you. These twists form the two headhunters.

Draw the hands slowly apart and the headhunters will move toward each other. Then, by jerking the left hand strings, they can be made to fight. The result of the contest is uncertain. Either "they kill each other," according to the natives, and fall apart; or "one may kill the other and travel home" toward the right hand, or Murray Island, taking his enemy's head along with him.

If you wish the Dauar Island man to win and run off to the left, start Opening A by taking up the right palm string first. Then, when the figure is completed, pull on the right near strings, and the victorious headhunter will run off to the left.

THE LEASHING OF LOCHIEL'S DOGS

THIS string game is well known in England, Scotland and Ireland, and it has also been found among the Cherokees and the natives of Africa and Australia. In some parts of Ireland it is known as "Duck's Feet" and in the Hebrides Islands, it is called "Tying the Dogs."

Start with Opening A.

Turn the palms toward you and close the four fingers over all the strings except the near thumb string. Turn both hands down, pass them under the near thumb string, and return the hands to a vertical position. This will cause the near thumb string to slip over the fingers to the far side of the hand.

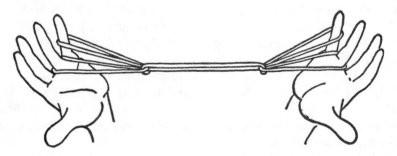

With the thumb and forefinger of the right hand, remove the loop from the left forefinger and put it on the left thumb. With the thumb and forefinger of the left hand, remove the loop from the right forefinger and put it on the right thumb.

With the thumb and forefinger of the right hand, take the string on the back of the left hand and put it on the left middle finger. With the thumb and forefinger of the left hand, take the string on the back of the right hand and put it on the right middle finger. Draw the strings tight by separating the hands.

Turn the palms toward you, bend the little fingers down over the far middle finger strings, and pick up from below on the backs of the little fingers the near little finger strings. Return the little fingers to their former upright positions.

With the thumb and forefinger of the right hand, take the lower left far little string—the one that stretches straight across to the right little finger—lift it over the tip of the left little finger, and drop it on the palm side of the little finger. In the same way pick up the lower right far little finger string with the left thumb and forefinger and lift it over the tip of the right little finger. Draw the hands apart.

Now release the thumbs from their loops and separate the hands to form the completed figure. Lochiel's Dogs are the middle and little fingers of each hand, and it will be seen that they are leashed securely by the loops that lead to the two central strings.

THE SETTING SUN

THIS is a very interesting figure from the Torres Straits. The movements are easy, but quite a long string should be used to allow for sufficient room for the fingers to move in while making the last movement or two.

Start with Opening A.

Bend the little fingers toward you over all the strings except the near thumb string. Put the little fingers down into the thumb loop, pick up on their backs the near thumb string, and return the little fingers to their original positions. The thumb loop should be taken entirely off the thumbs by this movement.

Pass each thumb away from you under the forefinger loops, and take up from below on the backs of the thumbs the two near little finger strings. Return the thumbs to their positions.

Release the loops from the little fingers.

Bend each little finger toward you over the forefinger loops, and pick up from below on the backs of the fingers the two far thumb strings. Return the little fingers to their positions.

Now exchange the loops on the forefingers by bringing the hands close together and putting the right forefinger loop on the left fore-finger and then putting the left forefinger loop on the right fore-finger. This passes the right forefinger loop down through the left forefinger loop.

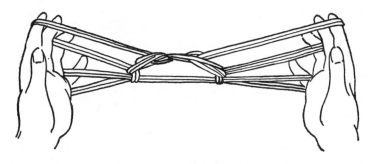

Bend the two middle fingers down and put them from above into the forefinger loops. Pick up from below on the backs of the middle fingers the two far thumb strings and return the middle fingers back through the forefinger loops to their original positions. (The thumb and forefinger of the opposite hand can be used to help put the far thumb strings on the back of each middle finger, and can also assist in getting the fingers back through the forefinger loops.)

Release the loops on the thumbs and forefingers. Then transfer the two loops on the middle fingers to the thumbs of the same hands.

In the center of the figure there is now a small triangle with its base on the far side of the figure. The base is formed by the two strings that pass from one little finger to the other. The two sides of the triangle are formed by the two near thumb strings. Pick up from below on the back of each forefinger the strings forming the sides of the triangle. The right forefinger picks up the right side and the left forefinger the left side. Return the forefingers to their upright positions.

Put the two middle fingers from above through the two forefinger loops and pick up from below on the backs of the middle fingers the two far thumb strings.   Return the middle fingers, through the two forefinger loops, to their upright positions.   (Use the opposite hands, if desired, to help in executing this movement.)

Release the loops from the thumbs and forefingers.   Keep the loops on the little fingers and extend the figure by putting the two forefingers into the middle finger loops to widen them out.

The figure shows the sun halfway beneath the horizon, with rays shooting upward on either side.   The rays can be made more numerous by transferring one of the middle finger loops on each hand to the forefinger of the hand.   Release the loops on the forefingers and middle fingers, draw the hands apart, and the sun will set.

OSAGE INDIAN DIAMONDS

THIS is a beautiful and symmetrical Osage Indian figure, which is also found in the Hawaiian Islands.   It is sometimes known, among the Indians, as "Jacob's Ladder."

Start with Opening A.

Release the loops from the thumbs and draw the hands apart.

Pass the thumbs away from you beneath all the strings, and pick up, from below, on the backs of the thumbs the far little finger string. Return the thumbs to their original positions.

Pass the thumbs away from you over the near forefinger strings, and pick up, from below, on the backs of the thumbs the far forefinger strings.   Return the thumbs to their former positions.

Release the loops from the little fingers and draw the hands apart.

Pass the little fingers toward you over the near forefinger strings and pick up, from below, on the backs of the little fingers the far thumb strings.   Return the little fingers to their original positions.

Release the loops from the thumbs.

Pass the thumbs away from you over the forefinger loops and pick up, from below, on the backs of the thumbs the near little finger strings.   Return the thumbs to their former positions.

With the right thumb and forefinger, pick up the left near forefinger string close to the forefinger and between it and the left palm string. Put the left near forefinger string over the left thumb. Pick up the right near forefinger string in the same way with the left thumb and forefinger and put it over the right thumb. Separate the hands.

Remove the lower near thumb string by bending down the thumbs and letting the string slip over them to the far side. Do not let this disturb the upper thumb loop.

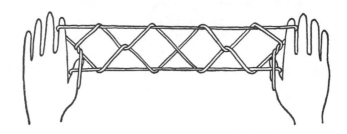

Put the forefingers from above down into the small triangles formed by the palm strings twisting around the thumb loops. Turn the palms down and release the loops on the little fingers. Separate the hands slowly, turning the palms away from you, and the four "Osage Diamonds" will make their appearance.

BAGOBO DIAMONDS

THIS is an interesting diamond figure that comes from the Bagobo Tribe in the Philippine Islands.

Start with Opening A. The *left* palm string *must* be taken up first.

Release the loops from the little fingers.

Transfer the thumb loops to the forefingers by bending down the forefingers and inserting them from below into the thumb loops.

Pass the thumbs away from you over the lower near forefinger strings and with the backs of the thumbs pick up, from below, the lower far forefinger strings. Return the thumbs to their original positions.

Pass the thumbs away from you over the upper near forefinger strings and with the backs of the thumbs pick up, from below, the upper far forefinger strings. Return the thumbs to their original positions.

Bring the ring fingers toward you over the upper near forefinger strings and pick up, from below, on the backs of the ring fingers, the lower near forefinger strings.

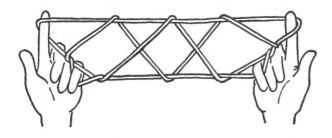

Lift the two lower near thumb strings over the tips of the thumbs, allowing them to drop on the palm sides of the thumbs. The easiest way to lift these strings over the thumbs is to use the teeth.

Draw the strings tight. Move the left hand down and turn it palm up with the fingers pointing away from you. Turn the right hand palm-down and swing its fingers in toward you, as shown in the illustration, and the completed figure will appear.

THE SEA-COW

THIS is a Torres Straits figure which some of the natives believe bears a resemblance to the Dugong or sea-cow, while others call it a King Fish. It develops into a game or trick at the end.

Start with Opening A, and be sure to pick up the left palm string first.

Release the loop from the right forefinger. Separate the hands to draw the strings tight.

Bend the left forefinger down between the two forefinger strings and hold tightly, in the bend of the finger, the string that passes across the left palm from the ring finger to the thumb. Turn the left-hand palm down and with fingers pointing to the right, let all the strings slip off the left hand except the string held in the bend of the left forefinger. Pull this string to the left to pull all the strings tight.

Take the loop held by the left forefinger between the right thumb and forefinger and arrange it on the left hand in Position 1, crossing the palm and behind the little finger and thumb.

Bring the palms close together. Point the left forefinger down and put it, from above, behind or to the right of the string that crosses the right palm. With the left forefinger still pointing down, draw the string away from the palm. As you separate the hands, turn the left forefinger toward you and then upward. This twists the string around the left forefinger.

Bend the right forefinger down into the right thumb loop. Then, turning the palm away from you, put the right forefinger, carrying the right far thumb string, down into the little finger loop, and pick up with its tip the right near little finger string. As you return the forefinger to its original position the string which was the right far thumb string will slip off the forefinger. This entire movement might be described as pulling the near little finger string through the thumb loop with the right forefinger.

Bend the left little finger down into the left forefinger loop, close to the forefinger. Pull down and hold tightly the left far forefinger string.

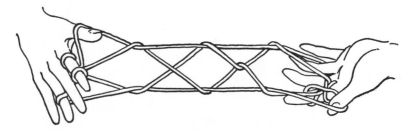

Bend the right little finger down over the right far thumb string. Pull this string down in the bend of the little finger.

Release the loops on the thumbs and draw the completed figure out between the forefinger and little finger of each hand. The strings on the forefingers must be kept well up toward the tips. If the figure does not come out well, it can be worked into shape by pushing toward the center the straight string running from the forefinger to the little finger on each hand.

The trick that goes with this figure is worked as follows: Tell one of your friends to put his hand through the central diamond of the figure. Then, at will, you can catch his wrist in the strings, or make the strings pass right through his wrist. To catch his wrist, drop the strings in your left hand and pull with your right hand. To make the strings pass through his wrist, drop the right-hand strings and pull with your left hand.

CHEATING THE HANGMAN

WHILE this is a string game that is well known to the natives of the Caroline and Philippine Islands, it can be included in any program of string magic. A story can be told about a magician who was condemned to be hanged but always succeeded, by the exercise of his magic powers, in slipping out of the hangman's noose.

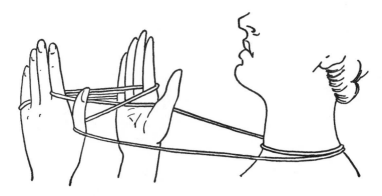

Take a long loop of string and put it over your head, allowing the free end to hang down in front of you. Pass the right-hand string around your neck, passing it from right to left. Then put your hands in the hanging loop in front of you and form Opening A, being sure to take up the left palm string first. Release the little fingers and put

the loop between the two forefingers over your head. Then pull on
the loop that hangs down in front of you and the string will apparently pass right through your neck and come away free.

THE SAWMILL

THIS game is played in England and Ireland and is known to
some extent in this country. It is a reproduction in string of a sawmill with a cross-cut saw busily at work cutting through a piece of
timber.

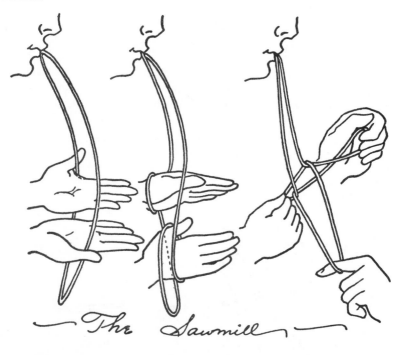

The Sawmill

Take a loop of string and hold one of its strings between the
teeth, allowing the rest of the loop to hang down in front of you. Put
the right and left hands, palms uppermost, into the loop, from the
near to the far side. Let the right string of the loop lie across the
palm of the right hand and the left string of the loop lie across the

palm of the left hand. Close the fingers of each hand on the palms over the strings and revolve the hands inwards. Open out the fingers and the strings will be looped around the hands, as shown in the center drawing. Each hand, if desired, can loop the string around the other hand, as shown, if it is found difficult to do the inward-turning movement.

Now exchange the loops on each hand, passing one loop through the other. Ask one of your friends to take hold of the hanging loop and pull it out. Then, by pulling alternately the loops held by the hands and the loops held by your teeth and by your friend, the sawing motion is produced.

BIBLIOGRAPHY

Artists in String, Kathleen Haddon; E. P. Dutton & Co., New York.

Bluejacket's Manual; Navy Department, Washington, D. C.

Braiding and Knotting For Amateurs, Constantine A. Belash; Beacon Press, Boston. (Dover Reprint)

Handicraft, Lester Griswold; Colorado Springs, Col.

Home Craft Rugs, Lydia L. Walker; F. A. Stokes Co., New York.

Homespun Handicrafts, Ella S. Bowles; J. B. Lippincott Co., Philadelphia.

How To Make Rugs, Candace Wheeler; Doubleday Page & Co., New York.

Illustrated Magic, Ottokar Fischer; The Macmillan Co., New York.

Knots, Splices and Fancy Work, Charles L. Spencer; Brown, Son and Ferguson, Glasgow.

Knots, Ties and Splices, Joseph Tom Burgess; Routledge, London.

Mathematical Recreations and Essays, W. W. R. Ball; The Macmillan Co., New York.

Sailors' Knots, Cyrus Lawrence Day; Dodd Mead & Co., New York.

Square Knot Book, P. C. Hertwig; P. C. Hertwig Co., Brooklyn.

String Figures, Caroline Furness Jayne; Chas. Scribners' Sons, New York. (Dover Reprint)
(This book contains directions for all the figures of Cat's Cradles.)

String Games For Beginners, Kathleen Haddon; W. Heffer & Sons, Cambridge.

Thirty-Three Rope Ties and Chain Releases, Burling Hull, New York.

Weaving and Other Pleasant Occupations, R. K. and M. I. R. Polkinghorne; George C. Harrap & Co., London.

A CATALOG OF SELECTED
DOVER BOOKS
IN ALL FIELDS OF INTEREST

A CATALOG OF SELECTED DOVER
BOOKS IN ALL FIELDS OF INTEREST

CONCERNING THE SPIRITUAL IN ART, Wassily Kandinsky. Pioneering work by father of abstract art. Thoughts on color theory, nature of art. Analysis of earlier masters. 12 illustrations. 80pp. of text. 5⅜ x 8½. 23411-8 Pa. $3.95

ANIMALS: 1,419 Copyright-Free Illustrations of Mammals, Birds, Fish, Insects, etc., Jim Harter (ed.). Clear wood engravings present, in extremely lifelike poses, over 1,000 species of animals. One of the most extensive pictorial sourcebooks of its kind. Captions. Index. 284pp. 9 x 12. 23766-4 Pa. $12.95

CELTIC ART: The Methods of Construction, George Bain. Simple geometric techniques for making Celtic interlacements, spirals, Kells-type initials, animals, humans, etc. Over 500 illustrations. 160pp. 9 x 12. (USO) 22923-8 Pa. $9.95

AN ATLAS OF ANATOMY FOR ARTISTS, Fritz Schider. Most thorough reference work on art anatomy in the world. Hundreds of illustrations, including selections from works by Vesalius, Leonardo, Goya, Ingres, Michelangelo, others. 593 illustrations. 192pp. 7⅛ x 10¼. 20241-0 Pa. $9 95

CELTIC HAND STROKE-BY-STROKE (Irish Half-Uncial from "The Book of Kells"): An Arthur Baker Calligraphy Manual, Arthur Baker. Complete guide to creating each letter of the alphabet in distinctive Celtic manner. Covers hand position, strokes, pens, inks, paper, more. Illustrated. 48pp. 8¼ x 11. 24336-2 Pa. $3.95

EASY ORIGAMI, John Montroll. Charming collection of 32 projects (hat, cup, pelican, piano, swan, many more) specially designed for the novice origami hobbyist. Clearly illustrated easy-to-follow instructions insure that even beginning papercrafters will achieve successful results. 48pp. 8¼ x 11. 27298-2 Pa. $2.95

THE COMPLETE BOOK OF BIRDHOUSE CONSTRUCTION FOR WOOD-WORKERS, Scott D. Campbell. Detailed instructions, illustrations, tables. Also data on bird habitat and instinct patterns. Bibliography. 3 tables. 63 illustrations in 15 figures. 48pp. 5¼ x 8½. 24407-5 Pa. $2.50

BLOOMINGDALE'S ILLUSTRATED 1886 CATALOG: Fashions, Dry Goods and Housewares, Bloomingdale Brothers. Famed merchants' extremely rare catalog depicting about 1,700 products: clothing, housewares, firearms, dry goods, jewelry, more. Invaluable for dating, identifying vintage items. Also, copyright-free graphics for artists, designers. Co-published with Henry Ford Museum & Greenfield Village. 160pp. 8¼ x 11. 25780-0 Pa. $9.95

HISTORIC COSTUME IN PICTURES, Braun & Schneider. Over 1,450 costumed figures in clearly detailed engravings–from dawn of civilization to end of 19th century. Captions. Many folk costumes. 256pp. 8⅜ x 11¾. 23150-X Pa. $12.95

STICKLEY CRAFTSMAN FURNITURE CATALOGS, Gustav Stickley and L. & J. G. Stickley. Beautiful, functional furniture in two authentic catalogs from 1910. 594 illustrations, including 277 photos, show settles, rockers, armchairs, reclining chairs, bookcases, desks, tables. 183pp. 6½ x 9¼. 23838-5 Pa. $9.95

AMERICAN LOCOMOTIVES IN HISTORIC PHOTOGRAPHS: 1858 to 1949, Ron Ziel (ed.). A rare collection of 126 meticulously detailed official photographs, called "builder portraits," of American locomotives that majestically chronicle the rise of steam locomotive power in America. Introduction. Detailed captions. xi + 129pp. 9 x 12. 27393-8 Pa. $12.95

AMERICA'S LIGHTHOUSES: An Illustrated History, Francis Ross Holland, Jr. Delightfully written, profusely illustrated fact-filled survey of over 200 American lighthouses since 1716. History, anecdotes, technological advances, more. 240pp. 8 x 10¾. 25576-X Pa. $12.95

TOWARDS A NEW ARCHITECTURE, Le Corbusier. Pioneering manifesto by founder of "International School." Technical and aesthetic theories, views of industry, economics, relation of form to function, "mass-production split" and much more. Profusely illustrated. 320pp. 6⅛ x 9¼. (USO) 25023-7 Pa. $9.95

HOW THE OTHER HALF LIVES, Jacob Riis. Famous journalistic record, exposing poverty and degradation of New York slums around 1900, by major social reformer. 100 striking and influential photographs. 233pp. 10 x 7⅞. 22012-5 Pa. $10.95

FRUIT KEY AND TWIG KEY TO TREES AND SHRUBS, William M. Harlow. One of the handiest and most widely used identification aids. Fruit key covers 120 deciduous and evergreen species; twig key 160 deciduous species. Easily used. Over 300 photographs. 126pp. 5⅜ x 8½. 20511-8 Pa. $3.95

COMMON BIRD SONGS, Dr. Donald J. Borror. Songs of 60 most common U.S. birds: robins, sparrows, cardinals, bluejays, finches, more–arranged in order of increasing complexity. Up to 9 variations of songs of each species. Cassette and manual 99911-4 $8.95

ORCHIDS AS HOUSE PLANTS, Rebecca Tyson Northen. Grow cattleyas and many other kinds of orchids–in a window, in a case, or under artificial light. 63 illustrations. 148pp. 5⅜ x 8½. 23261-1 Pa. $4.95

MONSTER MAZES, Dave Phillips. Masterful mazes at four levels of difficulty. Avoid deadly perils and evil creatures to find magical treasures. Solutions for all 32 exciting illustrated puzzles. 48pp. 8¼ x 11. 26005-4 Pa. $2.95

MOZART'S DON GIOVANNI (DOVER OPERA LIBRETTO SERIES), Wolfgang Amadeus Mozart. Introduced and translated by Ellen H. Bleiler. Standard Italian libretto, with complete English translation. Convenient and thoroughly portable–an ideal companion for reading along with a recording or the performance itself. Introduction. List of characters. Plot summary. 121pp. 5¼ x 8½. 24944-1 Pa. $2.95

TECHNICAL MANUAL AND DICTIONARY OF CLASSICAL BALLET, Gail Grant. Defines, explains, comments on steps, movements, poses and concepts. 15-page pictorial section. Basic book for student, viewer. 127pp. 5⅜ x 8½. 21843-0 Pa. $4.95

BRASS INSTRUMENTS: Their History and Development, Anthony Baines. Authoritative, updated survey of the evolution of trumpets, trombones, bugles, cornets, French horns, tubas and other brass wind instruments. Over 140 illustrations and 48 music examples. Corrected and updated by author. New preface. Bibliography. 320pp. 5⅜ x 8½. 27574-4 Pa. $9.95

HOLLYWOOD GLAMOR PORTRAITS, John Kobal (ed.). 145 photos from 1926-49. Harlow, Gable, Bogart, Bacall; 94 stars in all. Full background on photographers, technical aspects. 160pp. 8⅜ x 11¼. 23352-9 Pa. $11.95

MAX AND MORITZ, Wilhelm Busch. Great humor classic in both German and English. Also 10 other works: "Cat and Mouse," "Plisch and Plumm," etc. 216pp. 5⅜ x 8½. 20181-3 Pa. $6.95

THE RAVEN AND OTHER FAVORITE POEMS, Edgar Allan Poe. Over 40 of the author's most memorable poems: "The Bells," "Ulalume," "Israfel," "To Helen," "The Conqueror Worm," "Eldorado," "Annabel Lee," many more. Alphabetic lists of titles and first lines. 64pp. 5³⁄₁₆ x 8¼. 26685-0 Pa. $1.00

PERSONAL MEMOIRS OF U. S. GRANT, Ulysses Simpson Grant. Intelligent, deeply moving firsthand account of Civil War campaigns, considered by many the finest military memoirs ever written. Includes letters, historic photographs, maps and more. 528pp. 6⅛ x 9¼. 28587-1 Pa. $11.95

AMULETS AND SUPERSTITIONS, E. A. Wallis Budge. Comprehensive discourse on origin, powers of amulets in many ancient cultures: Arab, Persian Babylonian, Assyrian, Egyptian, Gnostic, Hebrew, Phoenician, Syriac, etc. Covers cross, swastika, crucifix, seals, rings, stones, etc. 584pp. 5⅜ x 8½. 23573-4 Pa. $12.95

RUSSIAN STORIES/PYCCKNE PACCKA3bl: A Dual-Language Book, edited by Gleb Struve. Twelve tales by such masters as Chekhov, Tolstoy, Dostoevsky, Pushkin, others. Excellent word-for-word English translations on facing pages, plus teaching and study aids, Russian/English vocabulary, biographical/critical introductions, more. 416pp. 5⅜ x 8½. 26244-8 Pa. $8.95

PHILADELPHIA THEN AND NOW: 60 Sites Photographed in the Past and Present, Kenneth Finkel and Susan Oyama. Rare photographs of City Hall, Logan Square, Independence Hall, Betsy Ross House, other landmarks juxtaposed with contemporary views. Captures changing face of historic city. Introduction. Captions. 128pp. 8¼ x 11. 25790-8 Pa. $9.95

AIA ARCHITECTURAL GUIDE TO NASSAU AND SUFFOLK COUNTIES, LONG ISLAND, The American Institute of Architects, Long Island Chapter, and the Society for the Preservation of Long Island Antiquities. Comprehensive, well-researched and generously illustrated volume brings to life over three centuries of Long Island's great architectural heritage. More than 240 photographs with authoritative, extensively detailed captions. 176pp. 8¼ x 11. 26946-9 Pa. $14.95

NORTH AMERICAN INDIAN LIFE: Customs and Traditions of 23 Tribes, Elsie Clews Parsons (ed.). 27 fictionalized essays by noted anthropologists examine religion, customs, government, additional facets of life among the Winnebago, Crow, Zuni, Eskimo, other tribes. 480pp. 6⅛ x 9¼. 27377-6 Pa. $10.95

FRANK LLOYD WRIGHT'S HOLLYHOCK HOUSE, Donald Hoffmann. Lavishly illustrated, carefully documented study of one of Wright's most controversial residential designs. Over 120 photographs, floor plans, elevations, etc. Detailed perceptive text by noted Wright scholar. Index. 128pp. 9¼ x 10¾. 27133-1 Pa. $11.95

THE MALE AND FEMALE FIGURE IN MOTION: 60 Classic Photographic Sequences, Eadweard Muybridge. 60 true-action photographs of men and women walking, running, climbing, bending, turning, etc., reproduced from rare 19th-century masterpiece. vi + 121pp. 9 x 12. 24745-7 Pa. $10.95

1001 QUESTIONS ANSWERED ABOUT THE SEASHORE, N. J. Berrill and Jacquelyn Berrill. Queries answered about dolphins, sea snails, sponges, starfish, fishes, shore birds, many others. Covers appearance, breeding, growth, feeding, much more. 305pp. 5¼ x 8¼. 23366-9 Pa. $8.95

GUIDE TO OWL WATCHING IN NORTH AMERICA, Donald S. Heintzelman. Superb guide offers complete data and descriptions of 19 species: barn owl, screech owl, snowy owl, many more. Expert coverage of owl-watching equipment, conservation, migrations and invasions, etc. Guide to observing sites. 84 illustrations. xiii + 193pp. 5⅜ x 8½. 27344-X Pa. $8.95

MEDICINAL AND OTHER USES OF NORTH AMERICAN PLANTS: A Historical Survey with Special Reference to the Eastern Indian Tribes, Charlotte Erichsen-Brown. Chronological historical citations document 500 years of usage of plants, trees, shrubs native to eastern Canada, northeastern U.S. Also complete identifying information. 343 illustrations. 544pp. 6½ x 9¼. 25951-X Pa. $12.95

STORYBOOK MAZES, Dave Phillips. 23 stories and mazes on two-page spreads: Wizard of Oz, Treasure Island, Robin Hood, etc. Solutions. 64pp. 8¼ x 11. 23628-5 Pa. $2.95

NEGRO FOLK MUSIC, U.S.A., Harold Courlander. Noted folklorist's scholarly yet readable analysis of rich and varied musical tradition. Includes authentic versions of over 40 folk songs. Valuable bibliography and discography. xi + 324pp. 5⅜ x 8½. 27350-4 Pa. $7.95

MOVIE-STAR PORTRAITS OF THE FORTIES, John Kobal (ed.). 163 glamor, studio photos of 106 stars of the 1940s: Rita Hayworth, Ava Gardner, Marlon Brando, Clark Gable, many more. 176pp. 8⅜ x 11¼. 23546-7 Pa. $12.95

BENCHLEY LOST AND FOUND, Robert Benchley. Finest humor from early 30s, about pet peeves, child psychologists, post office and others. Mostly unavailable elsewhere. 73 illustrations by Peter Arno and others. 183pp. 5⅜ x 8½. 22410-4 Pa. $6.95

YEKL and THE IMPORTED BRIDEGROOM AND OTHER STORIES OF YIDDISH NEW YORK, Abraham Cahan. Film Hester Street based on Yekl (1896). Novel, other stories among first about Jewish immigrants on N.Y.'s East Side. 240pp. 5⅜ x 8½. 22427-9 Pa. $6.95

SELECTED POEMS, Walt Whitman. Generous sampling from *Leaves of Grass*. Twenty-four poems include "I Hear America Singing," "Song of the Open Road," "I Sing the Body Electric," "When Lilacs Last in the Dooryard Bloom'd," "O Captain! My Captain!"–all reprinted from an authoritative edition. Lists of titles and first lines. 128pp. 5³⁄₁₆ x 8¼. 26878-0 Pa. $1.00

THE BEST TALES OF HOFFMANN, E. T. A. Hoffmann. 10 of Hoffmann's most important stories: "Nutcracker and the King of Mice," "The Golden Flowerpot," etc. 458pp. 5⅜ x 8½. 21793-0 Pa. $9.95

FROM FETISH TO GOD IN ANCIENT EGYPT, E. A. Wallis Budge. Rich detailed survey of Egyptian conception of "God" and gods, magic, cult of animals, Osiris, more. Also, superb English translations of hymns and legends. 240 illustrations. 545pp. 5⅜ x 8½. 25803-3 Pa. $11.95

FRENCH STORIES/CONTES FRANÇAIS: A Dual-Language Book, Wallace Fowlie. Ten stories by French masters, Voltaire to Camus: "Micromegas" by Voltaire; "The Atheist's Mass" by Balzac; "Minuet" by de Maupassant; "The Guest" by Camus, six more. Excellent English translations on facing pages. Also French-English vocabulary list, exercises, more. 352pp. 5⅜ x 8½. 26443-2 Pa. $8.95

CHICAGO AT THE TURN OF THE CENTURY IN PHOTOGRAPHS: 122 Historic Views from the Collections of the Chicago Historical Society, Larry A. Viskochil. Rare large-format prints offer detailed views of City Hall, State Street, the Loop, Hull House, Union Station, many other landmarks, circa 1904-1913. Introduction. Captions. Maps. 144pp. 9⅜ x 12¼. 24656-6 Pa. $12.95

OLD BROOKLYN IN EARLY PHOTOGRAPHS, 1865-1929, William Lee Younger. Luna Park, Gravesend race track, construction of Grand Army Plaza, moving of Hotel Brighton, etc. 157 previously unpublished photographs. 165pp. 8⅞ x 11¾. 23587-4 Pa. $13.95

THE MYTHS OF THE NORTH AMERICAN INDIANS, Lewis Spence. Rich anthology of the myths and legends of the Algonquins, Iroquois, Pawnees and Sioux, prefaced by an extensive historical and ethnological commentary. 36 illustrations. 480pp. 5⅜ x 8½. 25967-6 Pa. $8.95

AN ENCYCLOPEDIA OF BATTLES: Accounts of Over 1,560 Battles from 1479 B.C. to the Present, David Eggenberger. Essential details of every major battle in recorded history from the first battle of Megiddo in 1479 B.C. to Grenada in 1984. List of Battle Maps. New Appendix covering the years 1967-1984. Index. 99 illustrations. 544pp. 6½ x 9¼. 24913-1 Pa. $14.95

SAILING ALONE AROUND THE WORLD, Captain Joshua Slocum. First man to sail around the world, alone, in small boat. One of great feats of seamanship told in delightful manner. 67 illustrations. 294pp. 5⅜ x 8½. 20326-3 Pa. $5.95

ANARCHISM AND OTHER ESSAYS, Emma Goldman. Powerful, penetrating, prophetic essays on direct action, role of minorities, prison reform, puritan hypocrisy, violence, etc. 271pp. 5⅜ x 8½. 22484-8 Pa. $6.95

MYTHS OF THE HINDUS AND BUDDHISTS, Ananda K. Coomaraswamy and Sister Nivedita. Great stories of the epics; deeds of Krishna, Shiva, taken from puranas, Vedas, folk tales; etc. 32 illustrations. 400pp. 5⅜ x 8½. 21759-0 Pa. $10.95

BEYOND PSYCHOLOGY, Otto Rank. Fear of death, desire of immortality, nature of sexuality, social organization, creativity, according to Rankian system. 291pp. 5⅜ x 8½. 20485-5 Pa. $8.95

A THEOLOGICO-POLITICAL TREATISE, Benedict Spinoza. Also contains unfinished Political Treatise. Great classic on religious liberty, theory of government on common consent. R. Elwes translation. Total of 421pp. 5⅜ x 8½. 20249-6 Pa. $9.95

MY BONDAGE AND MY FREEDOM, Frederick Douglass. Born a slave, Douglass became outspoken force in antislavery movement. The best of Douglass' autobiographies. Graphic description of slave life. 464pp. 5⅜ x 8½. 22457-0 Pa. $8.95

FOLLOWING THE EQUATOR: A Journey Around the World, Mark Twain. Fascinating humorous account of 1897 voyage to Hawaii, Australia, India, New Zealand, etc. Ironic, bemused reports on peoples, customs, climate, flora and fauna, politics, much more. 197 illustrations. 720pp. 5⅜ x 8½. 26113-1 Pa. $15.95

THE PEOPLE CALLED SHAKERS, Edward D. Andrews. Definitive study of Shakers: origins, beliefs, practices, dances, social organization, furniture and crafts, etc. 33 illustrations. 351pp. 5⅜ x 8½. 21081-2 Pa. $8.95

THE MYTHS OF GREECE AND ROME, H. A. Guerber. A classic of mythology, generously illustrated, long prized for its simple, graphic, accurate retelling of the principal myths of Greece and Rome, and for its commentary on their origins and significance. With 64 illustrations by Michelangelo, Raphael, Titian, Rubens, Canova, Bernini and others. 480pp. 5⅜ x 8½. 27584-1 Pa. $9.95

PSYCHOLOGY OF MUSIC, Carl E. Seashore. Classic work discusses music as a medium from psychological viewpoint. Clear treatment of physical acoustics, auditory apparatus, sound perception, development of musical skills, nature of musical feeling, host of other topics. 88 figures. 408pp. 5⅜ x 8½. 21851-1 Pa. $10.95

THE PHILOSOPHY OF HISTORY, Georg W. Hegel. Great classic of Western thought develops concept that history is not chance but rational process, the evolution of freedom. 457pp. 5⅜ x 8½. 20112-0 Pa. $9.95

THE BOOK OF TEA, Kakuzo Okakura. Minor classic of the Orient: entertaining, charming explanation, interpretation of traditional Japanese culture in terms of tea ceremony. 94pp. 5⅜ x 8½. 20070-1 Pa. $3.95

LIFE IN ANCIENT EGYPT, Adolf Erman. Fullest, most thorough, detailed older account with much not in more recent books, domestic life, religion, magic, medicine, commerce, much more. Many illustrations reproduce tomb paintings, carvings, hieroglyphs, etc. 597pp. 5⅜ x 8½. 22632-8 Pa. $11.95

SUNDIALS, Their Theory and Construction, Albert Waugh. Far and away the best, most thorough coverage of ideas, mathematics concerned, types, construction, adjusting anywhere. Simple, nontechnical treatment allows even children to build several of these dials. Over 100 illustrations. 230pp. 5⅜ x 8½. 22947-5 Pa. $7.95

DYNAMICS OF FLUIDS IN POROUS MEDIA, Jacob Bear. For advanced students of ground water hydrology, soil mechanics and physics, drainage and irrigation engineering, and more. 335 illustrations. Exercises, with answers. 784pp. 6⅛ x 9¼. 65675-6 Pa. $19.95

SONGS OF EXPERIENCE: Facsimile Reproduction with 26 Plates in Full Color, William Blake. 26 full-color plates from a rare 1826 edition. Includes "TheTyger," "London," "Holy Thursday," and other poems. Printed text of poems. 48pp. 5¼ x 7. 24636-1 Pa. $4.95

OLD-TIME VIGNETTES IN FULL COLOR, Carol Belanger Grafton (ed.). Over 390 charming, often sentimental illustrations, selected from archives of Victorian graphics—pretty women posing, children playing, food, flowers, kittens and puppies, smiling cherubs, birds and butterflies, much more. All copyright-free. 48pp. 9¼ x 12¼. 27269-9 Pa. $5.95

PERSPECTIVE FOR ARTISTS, Rex Vicat Cole. Depth, perspective of sky and sea, shadows, much more, not usually covered. 391 diagrams, 81 reproductions of drawings and paintings. 279pp. 5⅜ x 8½. 22487-2 Pa. $6.95

DRAWING THE LIVING FIGURE, Joseph Sheppard. Innovative approach to artistic anatomy focuses on specifics of surface anatomy, rather than muscles and bones. Over 170 drawings of live models in front, back and side views, and in widely varying poses. Accompanying diagrams. 177 illustrations. Introduction. Index. 144pp. 8⅜ x11¼. 26723-7 Pa. $8.95

GOTHIC AND OLD ENGLISH ALPHABETS: 100 Complete Fonts, Dan X. Solo. Add power, elegance to posters, signs, other graphics with 100 stunning copyright-free alphabets: Blackstone, Dolbey, Germania, 97 more–including many lower-case, numerals, punctuation marks. 104pp. 8⅛ x 11. 24695-7 Pa. $8.95

HOW TO DO BEADWORK, Mary White. Fundamental book on craft from simple projects to five-bead chains and woven works. 106 illustrations. 142pp. 5⅜ x 8. 20697-1 Pa. $4.95

THE BOOK OF WOOD CARVING, Charles Marshall Sayers. Finest book for beginners discusses fundamentals and offers 34 designs. "Absolutely first rate . . . well thought out and well executed."–E. J. Tangerman. 118pp. 7¾ x 10⅝. 23654-4 Pa. $6.95

ILLUSTRATED CATALOG OF CIVIL WAR MILITARY GOODS: Union Army Weapons, Insignia, Uniform Accessories, and Other Equipment, Schuyler, Hartley, and Graham. Rare, profusely illustrated 1846 catalog includes Union Army uniform and dress regulations, arms and ammunition, coats, insignia, flags, swords, rifles, etc. 226 illustrations. 160pp. 9 x 12. 24939-5 Pa. $10.95

WOMEN'S FASHIONS OF THE EARLY 1900s: An Unabridged Republication of "New York Fashions, 1909," National Cloak & Suit Co. Rare catalog of mail-order fashions documents women's and children's clothing styles shortly after the turn of the century. Captions offer full descriptions, prices. Invaluable resource for fashion, costume historians. Approximately 725 illustrations. 128pp. 8⅜ x 11¼. 27276-1 Pa. $11.95

THE 1912 AND 1915 GUSTAV STICKLEY FURNITURE CATALOGS, Gustav Stickley. With over 200 detailed illustrations and descriptions, these two catalogs are essential reading and reference materials and identification guides for Stickley furniture. Captions cite materials, dimensions and prices. 112pp. 6½ x 9¼. 26676-1 Pa. $9.95

EARLY AMERICAN LOCOMOTIVES, John H. White, Jr. Finest locomotive engravings from early 19th century: historical (1804–74), main-line (after 1870), special, foreign, etc. 147 plates. 142pp. 11⅜ x 8¼. 22772-3 Pa. $10.95

THE TALL SHIPS OF TODAY IN PHOTOGRAPHS, Frank O. Braynard. Lavishly illustrated tribute to nearly 100 majestic contemporary sailing vessels: Amerigo Vespucci, Clearwater, Constitution, Eagle, Mayflower, Sea Cloud, Victory, many more. Authoritative captions provide statistics, background on each ship. 190 black-and-white photographs and illustrations. Introduction. 128pp. 8⅞ x 11¾. 27163-3 Pa. $13.95

EARLY NINETEENTH-CENTURY CRAFTS AND TRADES, Peter Stockham (ed.). Extremely rare 1807 volume describes to youngsters the crafts and trades of the day: brickmaker, weaver, dressmaker, bookbinder, ropemaker, saddler, many more. Quaint prose, charming illustrations for each craft. 20 black-and-white line illustrations. 192pp. 4⅝ x 6. 27293-1 Pa. $4.95

VICTORIAN FASHIONS AND COSTUMES FROM HARPER'S BAZAR, 1867–1898, Stella Blum (ed.). Day costumes, evening wear, sports clothes, shoes, hats, other accessories in over 1,000 detailed engravings. 320pp. 9⅜ x 12¼.
22990-4 Pa. $14.95

GUSTAV STICKLEY, THE CRAFTSMAN, Mary Ann Smith. Superb study surveys broad scope of Stickley's achievement, especially in architecture. Design philosophy, rise and fall of the Craftsman empire, descriptions and floor plans for many Craftsman houses, more. 86 black-and-white halftones. 31 line illustrations. Introduction 208pp. 6½ x 9¼. 27210-9 Pa. $9.95

THE LONG ISLAND RAIL ROAD IN EARLY PHOTOGRAPHS, Ron Ziel. Over 220 rare photos, informative text document origin (1844) and development of rail service on Long Island. Vintage views of early trains, locomotives, stations, passengers, crews, much more. Captions. 8⅞ x 11¾. 26301-0 Pa. $13.95

THE BOOK OF OLD SHIPS: From Egyptian Galleys to Clipper Ships, Henry B. Culver. Superb, authoritative history of sailing vessels, with 80 magnificent line illustrations. Galley, bark, caravel, longship, whaler, many more. Detailed, informative text on each vessel by noted naval historian. Introduction. 256pp. 5⅜ x 8½.
27332-6 Pa. $7.95

TEN BOOKS ON ARCHITECTURE, Vitruvius. The most important book ever written on architecture. Early Roman aesthetics, technology, classical orders, site selection, all other aspects. Morgan translation. 331pp. 5⅜ x 8½. 20645-9 Pa. $8.95

THE HUMAN FIGURE IN MOTION, Eadweard Muybridge. More than 4,500 stopped-action photos, in action series, showing undraped men, women, children jumping, lying down, throwing, sitting, wrestling, carrying, etc. 390pp. 7⅞ x 10⅝.
20204-6 Clothbd. $25.95

TREES OF THE EASTERN AND CENTRAL UNITED STATES AND CANADA, William M. Harlow. Best one-volume guide to 140 trees. Full descriptions, woodlore, range, etc. Over 600 illustrations. Handy size. 288pp. 4½ x 6⅜.
20395-6 Pa. $5.95

SONGS OF WESTERN BIRDS, Dr. Donald J. Borror. Complete song and call repertoire of 60 western species, including flycatchers, juncoes, cactus wrens, many more–includes fully illustrated booklet. Cassette and manual 99913-0 $8.95

GROWING AND USING HERBS AND SPICES, Milo Miloradovich. Versatile handbook provides all the information needed for cultivation and use of all the herbs and spices available in North America. 4 illustrations. Index. Glossary. 236pp. 5⅜ x 8½.
25058-X Pa. $6.95

BIG BOOK OF MAZES AND LABYRINTHS, Walter Shepherd. 50 mazes and labyrinths in all–classical, solid, ripple, and more–in one great volume. Perfect inexpensive puzzler for clever youngsters. Full solutions. 112pp. 8⅛ x 11.
22951-3 Pa. $4.95

PIANO TUNING, J. Cree Fischer. Clearest, best book for beginner, amateur. Simple repairs, raising dropped notes, tuning by easy method of flattened fifths. No previous skills needed. 4 illustrations. 201pp. 5⅜ x 8½. 23267-0 Pa. $6.95

A SOURCE BOOK IN THEATRICAL HISTORY, A. M. Nagler. Contemporary observers on acting, directing, make-up, costuming, stage props, machinery, scene design, from Ancient Greece to Chekhov. 611pp. 5⅜ x 8½. 20515-0 Pa. $12.95

THE COMPLETE NONSENSE OF EDWARD LEAR, Edward Lear. All nonsense limericks, zany alphabets, Owl and Pussycat, songs, nonsense botany, etc., illustrated by Lear. Total of 320pp. 5⅜ x 8½. (USO) 20167-8 Pa. $6.95

VICTORIAN PARLOUR POETRY: An Annotated Anthology, Michael R. Turner. 117 gems by Longfellow, Tennyson, Browning, many lesser-known poets. "The Village Blacksmith," "Curfew Must Not Ring Tonight," "Only a Baby Small," dozens more, often difficult to find elsewhere. Index of poets, titles, first lines. xxiii + 325pp. 5⅜ x 8¼. 27044-0 Pa. $8.95

DUBLINERS, James Joyce. Fifteen stories offer vivid, tightly focused observations of the lives of Dublin's poorer classes. At least one, "The Dead," is considered a masterpiece. Reprinted complete and unabridged from standard edition. 160pp. 5³⁄₁₆ x 8¼. 26870-5 Pa. $1.00

THE HAUNTED MONASTERY and THE CHINESE MAZE MURDERS, Robert van Gulik. Two full novels by van Gulik, set in 7th-century China, continue adventures of Judge Dee and his companions. An evil Taoist monastery, seemingly supernatural events; overgrown topiary maze hides strange crimes. 27 illustrations. 328pp. 5⅜ x 8½. 23502-5 Pa. $8.95

THE BOOK OF THE SACRED MAGIC OF ABRAMELIN THE MAGE, translated by S. MacGregor Mathers. Medieval manuscript of ceremonial magic. Basic document in Aleister Crowley, Golden Dawn groups. 268pp. 5⅜ x 8½. 23211-5 Pa. $8.95

NEW RUSSIAN-ENGLISH AND ENGLISH-RUSSIAN DICTIONARY, M. A. O'Brien. This is a remarkably handy Russian dictionary, containing a surprising amount of information, including over 70,000 entries. 366pp. 4½ x 6⅛. 20208-9 Pa. $9.95

HISTORIC HOMES OF THE AMERICAN PRESIDENTS, Second, Revised Edition, Irvin Haas. A traveler's guide to American Presidential homes, most open to the public, depicting and describing homes occupied by every American President from George Washington to George Bush. With visiting hours, admission charges, travel routes. 175 photographs. Index. 160pp. 8¼ x 11. 26751-2 Pa. $11.95

NEW YORK IN THE FORTIES, Andreas Feininger. 162 brilliant photographs by the well-known photographer, formerly with *Life* magazine. Commuters, shoppers, Times Square at night, much else from city at its peak. Captions by John von Hartz. 181pp. 9¼ x 10¾. 23585-8 Pa. $12.95

INDIAN SIGN LANGUAGE, William Tomkins. Over 525 signs developed by Sioux and other tribes. Written instructions and diagrams. Also 290 pictographs. 111pp. 6⅛ x 9¼. 22029-X Pa. $3.95

ANATOMY: A Complete Guide for Artists, Joseph Sheppard. A master of figure drawing shows artists how to render human anatomy convincingly. Over 460 illustrations. 224pp. 8⅜ x 11¼. 27279-6 Pa. $10.95

MEDIEVAL CALLIGRAPHY: Its History and Technique, Marc Drogin. Spirited history, comprehensive instruction manual covers 13 styles (ca. 4th century thru 15th). Excellent photographs; directions for duplicating medieval techniques with modern tools. 224pp. 8⅜ x 11¼. 26142-5 Pa. $11.95

DRIED FLOWERS: How to Prepare Them, Sarah Whitlock and Martha Rankin. Complete instructions on how to use silica gel, meal and borax, perlite aggregate, sand and borax, glycerine and water to create attractive permanent flower arrangements. 12 illustrations. 32pp. 5⅜ x 8½. 21802-3 Pa. $1.00

EASY-TO-MAKE BIRD FEEDERS FOR WOODWORKERS, Scott D. Campbell. Detailed, simple-to-use guide for designing, constructing, caring for and using feeders. Text, illustrations for 12 classic and contemporary designs. 96pp. 5⅜ x 8½. 25847-5 Pa. $2.95

SCOTTISH WONDER TALES FROM MYTH AND LEGEND, Donald A. Mackenzie. 16 lively tales tell of giants rumbling down mountainsides, of a magic wand that turns stone pillars into warriors, of gods and goddesses, evil hags, powerful forces and more. 240pp. 5⅜ x 8½. 29677-6 Pa. $6.95

THE HISTORY OF UNDERCLOTHES, C. Willett Cunnington and Phyllis Cunnington. Fascinating, well-documented survey covering six centuries of English undergarments, enhanced with over 100 illustrations: 12th-century laced-up bodice, footed long drawers (1795), 19th-century bustles, 19th-century corsets for men, Victorian "bust improvers," much more. 272pp. 5⅝ x 8¼. 27124-2 Pa. $9.95

ARTS AND CRAFTS FURNITURE: The Complete Brooks Catalog of 1912, Brooks Manufacturing Co. Photos and detailed descriptions of more than 150 now very collectible furniture designs from the Arts and Crafts movement depict davenports, settees, buffets, desks, tables, chairs, bedsteads, dressers and more, all built of solid, quarter-sawed oak. Invaluable for students and enthusiasts of antiques, Americana and the decorative arts. 80pp. 6½ x 9¼. 27471-3 Pa. $7.95

HOW WE INVENTED THE AIRPLANE: An Illustrated History, Orville Wright. Fascinating firsthand account covers early experiments, construction of planes and motors, first flights, much more. Introduction and commentary by Fred C. Kelly. 76 photographs. 96pp. 8¼ x 11. 25662-6 Pa. $8.95

THE ARTS OF THE SAILOR: Knotting, Splicing and Ropework, Hervey Garrett Smith. Indispensable shipboard reference covers tools, basic knots and useful hitches; handsewing and canvas work, more. Over 100 illustrations. Delightful reading for sea lovers. 256pp. 5⅜ x 8½. 26440-8 Pa. $7.95

FRANK LLOYD WRIGHT'S FALLINGWATER: The House and Its History, Second, Revised Edition, Donald Hoffmann. A total revision–both in text and illustrations–of the standard document on Fallingwater, the boldest, most personal architectural statement of Wright's mature years, updated with valuable new material from the recently opened Frank Lloyd Wright Archives. "Fascinating"–*The New York Times.* 116 illustrations. 128pp. 9¼ x 10¾. 27430-6 Pa. $11.95

AUTOBIOGRAPHY: The Story of My Experiments with Truth, Mohandas K. Gandhi. Boyhood, legal studies, purification, the growth of the Satyagraha (nonviolent protest) movement. Critical, inspiring work of the man responsible for the freedom of India. 480pp. 5⅜ x 8½. (USO)   24593-4 Pa. $8.95

CELTIC MYTHS AND LEGENDS, T. W. Rolleston. Masterful retelling of Irish and Welsh stories and tales. Cuchulain, King Arthur, Deirdre, the Grail, many more. First paperback edition. 58 full-page illustrations. 512pp. 5⅜ x 8½.   26507-2 Pa. $9.95

THE PRINCIPLES OF PSYCHOLOGY, William James. Famous long course complete, unabridged. Stream of thought, time perception, memory, experimental methods; great work decades ahead of its time. 94 figures. 1,391pp. 5⅜ x 8½. 2-vol. set.
                                                          Vol. I: 20381-6 Pa. $12.95
                                                          Vol. II: 20382-4 Pa. $12.95

THE WORLD AS WILL AND REPRESENTATION, Arthur Schopenhauer. Definitive English translation of Schopenhauer's life work, correcting more than 1,000 errors, omissions in earlier translations. Translated by E. F. J. Payne. Total of 1,269pp. 5⅜ x 8½. 2-vol. set.   Vol. 1: 21761-2 Pa. $11.95
                                                          Vol. 2: 21762-0 Pa. $11.95

MAGIC AND MYSTERY IN TIBET, Madame Alexandra David-Neel. Experiences among lamas, magicians, sages, sorcerers, Bonpa wizards. A true psychic discovery. 32 illustrations. 321pp. 5⅜ x 8½. (USO)   22682-4 Pa. $8.95

THE EGYPTIAN BOOK OF THE DEAD, E. A. Wallis Budge. Complete reproduction of Ani's papyrus, finest ever found. Full hieroglyphic text, interlinear transliteration, word-for-word translation, smooth translation. 533pp. 6½ x 9¼.
                                                          21866-X Pa. $10.95

MATHEMATICS FOR THE NONMATHEMATICIAN, Morris Kline. Detailed, college-level treatment of mathematics in cultural and historical context, with numerous exercises. Recommended Reading Lists. Tables. Numerous figures. 641pp. 5⅜ x 8½.
                                                          24823-2 Pa. $11.95

THEORY OF WING SECTIONS: Including a Summary of Airfoil Data, Ira H. Abbott and A. E. von Doenhoff. Concise compilation of subsonic aerodynamic characteristics of NACA wing sections, plus description of theory. 350pp. of tables. 693pp. 5⅜ x 8½.   60586-8 Pa. $14.95

THE RIME OF THE ANCIENT MARINER, Gustave Doré, S. T. Coleridge. Doré's finest work; 34 plates capture moods, subtleties of poem. Flawless full-size reproductions printed on facing pages with authoritative text of poem. "Beautiful. Simply beautiful."–*Publisher's Weekly.* 77pp. 9¼ x 12.   22305-1 Pa. $6.95

NORTH AMERICAN INDIAN DESIGNS FOR ARTISTS AND CRAFTSPEO-PLE, Eva Wilson. Over 360 authentic copyright-free designs adapted from Navajo blankets, Hopi pottery, Sioux buffalo hides, more. Geometrics, symbolic figures, plant and animal motifs, etc. 128pp. 8⅜ x 11. (EUK)   25341-4 Pa. $8.95

SCULPTURE: Principles and Practice, Louis Slobodkin. Step-by-step approach to clay, plaster, metals, stone; classical and modern. 253 drawings, photos. 255pp. 8⅛ x 11.
                                                          22960-2 Pa. $10.95

PHOTOGRAPHIC SKETCHBOOK OF THE CIVIL WAR, Alexander Gardner. 100 photos taken on field during the Civil War. Famous shots of Manassas Harper's Ferry, Lincoln, Richmond, slave pens, etc. 244pp. 10⅝ x 8¼. 22731-6 Pa. $9.95

FIVE ACRES AND INDEPENDENCE, Maurice G. Kains. Great back-to-the-land classic explains basics of self-sufficient farming. The one book to get. 95 illustrations. 397pp. 5⅜ x 8½. 20974-1 Pa. $7.95

SONGS OF EASTERN BIRDS, Dr. Donald J. Borror. Songs and calls of 60 species most common to eastern U.S.: warblers, woodpeckers, flycatchers, thrushes, larks, many more in high-quality recording. Cassette and manual 99912-2 $8.95

A MODERN HERBAL, Margaret Grieve. Much the fullest, most exact, most useful compilation of herbal material. Gigantic alphabetical encyclopedia, from aconite to zedoary, gives botanical information, medical properties, folklore, economic uses, much else. Indispensable to serious reader. 161 illustrations. 888pp. 6½ x 9¼. 2-vol. set. (USO) Vol. I: 22798-7 Pa. $9.95
Vol. II: 22799-5 Pa. $9.95

HIDDEN TREASURE MAZE BOOK, Dave Phillips. Solve 34 challenging mazes accompanied by heroic tales of adventure. Evil dragons, people-eating plants, blood-thirsty giants, many more dangerous adversaries lurk at every twist and turn. 34 mazes, stories, solutions. 48pp. 8¼ x 11. 24566-7 Pa. $2.95

LETTERS OF W. A. MOZART, Wolfgang A. Mozart. Remarkable letters show bawdy wit, humor, imagination, musical insights, contemporary musical world; includes some letters from Leopold Mozart. 276pp. 5⅜ x 8½. 22859-2 Pa. $7.95

BASIC PRINCIPLES OF CLASSICAL BALLET, Agrippina Vaganova. Great Russian theoretician, teacher explains methods for teaching classical ballet. 118 illustrations. 175pp. 5⅜ x 8½. 22036-2 Pa. $5.95

THE JUMPING FROG, Mark Twain. Revenge edition. The original story of The Celebrated Jumping Frog of Calaveras County, a hapless French translation, and Twain's hilarious "retranslation" from the French. 12 illustrations. 66pp. 5⅜ x 8½. 22686-7 Pa. $3.95

BEST REMEMBERED POEMS, Martin Gardner (ed.). The 126 poems in this superb collection of 19th- and 20th-century British and American verse range from Shelley's "To a Skylark" to the impassioned "Renascence" of Edna St. Vincent Millay and to Edward Lear's whimsical "The Owl and the Pussycat." 224pp. 5⅜ x 8½. 27165-X Pa. $4.95

COMPLETE SONNETS, William Shakespeare. Over 150 exquisite poems deal with love, friendship, the tyranny of time, beauty's evanescence, death and other themes in language of remarkable power, precision and beauty. Glossary of archaic terms. 80pp. 5$\frac{3}{16}$ x 8¼. 26686-9 Pa. $1.00

BODIES IN A BOOKSHOP, R. T. Campbell. Challenging mystery of blackmail and murder with ingenious plot and superbly drawn characters. In the best tradition of British suspense fiction. 192pp. 5⅜ x 8½. 24720-1 Pa. $6.95

THE WIT AND HUMOR OF OSCAR WILDE, Alvin Redman (ed.). More than 1,000 ripostes, paradoxes, wisecracks: Work is the curse of the drinking classes; I can resist everything except temptation; etc. 258pp. 5⅜ x 8½.   20602-5 Pa. $5.95

SHAKESPEARE LEXICON AND QUOTATION DICTIONARY, Alexander Schmidt. Full definitions, locations, shades of meaning in every word in plays and poems. More than 50,000 exact quotations. 1,485pp. 6½ x 9¼. 2-vol. set.
Vol. 1: 22726-X Pa. $16.95
Vol. 2: 22727-8 Pa. $16.95

SELECTED POEMS, Emily Dickinson. Over 100 best-known, best-loved poems by one of America's foremost poets, reprinted from authoritative early editions. No comparable edition at this price. Index of first lines. 64pp. 5³⁄₁₆ x 8¼.
26466-1 Pa. $1.00

CELEBRATED CASES OF JUDGE DEE (DEE GOONG AN), translated by Robert van Gulik. Authentic 18th-century Chinese detective novel; Dee and associates solve three interlocked cases. Led to van Gulik's own stories with same characters. Extensive introduction. 9 illustrations. 237pp. 5⅜ x 8½.   23337-5 Pa. $6.95

THE MALLEUS MALEFICARUM OF KRAMER AND SPRENGER, translated by Montague Summers. Full text of most important witchhunter's "bible," used by both Catholics and Protestants. 278pp. 6⅝ x 10.   22802-9 Pa. $12.95

SPANISH STORIES/CUENTOS ESPAÑOLES: A Dual-Language Book, Angel Flores (ed.). Unique format offers 13 great stories in Spanish by Cervantes, Borges, others. Faithful English translations on facing pages. 352pp. 5⅜ x 8½.
25399-6 Pa. $8.95

THE CHICAGO WORLD'S FAIR OF 1893: A Photographic Record, Stanley Appelbaum (ed.). 128 rare photos show 200 buildings, Beaux-Arts architecture, Midway, original Ferris Wheel, Edison's kinetoscope, more. Architectural emphasis; full text. 116pp. 8¼ x 11.   23990-X Pa. $9.95

OLD QUEENS, N.Y., IN EARLY PHOTOGRAPHS, Vincent F. Seyfried and William Asadorian. Over 160 rare photographs of Maspeth, Jamaica, Jackson Heights, and other areas. Vintage views of DeWitt Clinton mansion, 1939 World's Fair and more. Captions. 192pp. 8⅞ x 11.   26358-4 Pa. $12.95

CAPTURED BY THE INDIANS: 15 Firsthand Accounts, 1750-1870, Frederick Drimmer. Astounding true historical accounts of grisly torture, bloody conflicts, relentless pursuits, miraculous escapes and more, by people who lived to tell the tale. 384pp. 5⅜ x 8½.   24901-8 Pa. $8.95

THE WORLD'S GREAT SPEECHES, Lewis Copeland and Lawrence W. Lamm (eds.). Vast collection of 278 speeches of Greeks to 1970. Powerful and effective models; unique look at history. 842pp. 5⅜ x 8½.   20468-5 Pa. $14.95

THE BOOK OF THE SWORD, Sir Richard F. Burton. Great Victorian scholar/adventurer's eloquent, erudite history of the "queen of weapons"—from prehistory to early Roman Empire. Evolution and development of early swords, variations (sabre, broadsword, cutlass, scimitar, etc.), much more. 336pp. 6⅛ x 9¼.
25434-8 Pa. $9.95

CATALOG OF DOVER BOOKS

THE INFLUENCE OF SEA POWER UPON HISTORY, 1660–1783, A. T. Mahan. Influential classic of naval history and tactics still used as text in war colleges. First paperback edition. 4 maps. 24 battle plans. 640pp. 5⅜ x 8½. 25509-3 Pa. $12.95

THE STORY OF THE TITANIC AS TOLD BY ITS SURVIVORS, Jack Winocour (ed.). What it was really like. Panic, despair, shocking inefficiency, and a little heroism. More thrilling than any fictional account. 26 illustrations. 320pp. 5⅜ x 8½. 20610-6 Pa. $8.95

FAIRY AND FOLK TALES OF THE IRISH PEASANTRY, William Butler Yeats (ed.). Treasury of 64 tales from the twilight world of Celtic myth and legend: "The Soul Cages," "The Kildare Pooka," "King O'Toole and his Goose," many more. Introduction and Notes by W. B. Yeats. 352pp. 5⅜ x 8½. 26941-8 Pa. $8.95

BUDDHIST MAHAYANA TEXTS, E. B. Cowell and Others (eds.). Superb, accurate translations of basic documents in Mahayana Buddhism, highly important in history of religions. The Buddha-karita of Asvaghosha, Larger Sukhavativyuha, more. 448pp. 5⅜ x 8½. 25552-2 Pa. $9.95

ONE TWO THREE . . . INFINITY: Facts and Speculations of Science, George Gamow. Great physicist's fascinating, readable overview of contemporary science: number theory, relativity, fourth dimension, entropy, genes, atomic structure, much more. 128 illustrations. Index. 352pp. 5⅜ x 8½. 25664-2 Pa. $8.95

ENGINEERING IN HISTORY, Richard Shelton Kirby, et al. Broad, nontechnical survey of history's major technological advances: birth of Greek science, industrial revolution, electricity and applied science, 20th-century automation, much more. 181 illustrations. ". . . excellent . . ."–*Isis.* Bibliography. vii + 530pp. 5⅜ x 8¼. 26412-2 Pa. $14.95

DALÍ ON MODERN ART: The Cuckolds of Antiquated Modern Art, Salvador Dalí. Influential painter skewers modern art and its practitioners. Outrageous evaluations of Picasso, Cézanne, Turner, more. 15 renderings of paintings discussed. 44 calligraphic decorations by Dalí. 96pp. 5⅜ x 8½. (USO) 29220-7 Pa. $4.95

ANTIQUE PLAYING CARDS: A Pictorial History, Henry René D'Allemagne. Over 900 elaborate, decorative images from rare playing cards (14th–20th centuries): Bacchus, death, dancing dogs, hunting scenes, royal coats of arms, players cheating, much more. 96pp. 9¼ x 12¼. 29265-7 Pa. $11.95

MAKING FURNITURE MASTERPIECES: 30 Projects with Measured Drawings, Franklin H. Gottshall. Step-by-step instructions, illustrations for constructing handsome, useful pieces, among them a Sheraton desk, Chippendale chair, Spanish desk, Queen Anne table and a William and Mary dressing mirror. 224pp. 8⅛ x 11¼. 29338-6 Pa. $13.95

THE FOSSIL BOOK: A Record of Prehistoric Life, Patricia V. Rich et al. Profusely illustrated definitive guide covers everything from single-celled organisms and dinosaurs to birds and mammals and the interplay between climate and man. Over 1,500 illustrations. 760pp. 7½ x 10⅛. 29371-8 Pa. $29.95

Prices subject to change without notice.

Available at your book dealer or write for free catalog to Dept. GI, Dover Publications, Inc., 31 East 2nd St., Mineola, N.Y. 11501. Dover publishes more than 500 books each year on science, elementary and advanced mathematics, biology, music, art, literary history, social sciences and other areas.